WILD THINGS TO MAKE

heirloom accessories and clothes
to sew for your children

Kirsty Hartley

WILD THINGS TO MAKE

heirloom accessories and clothes
to sew for your children

Kirsty Hartley

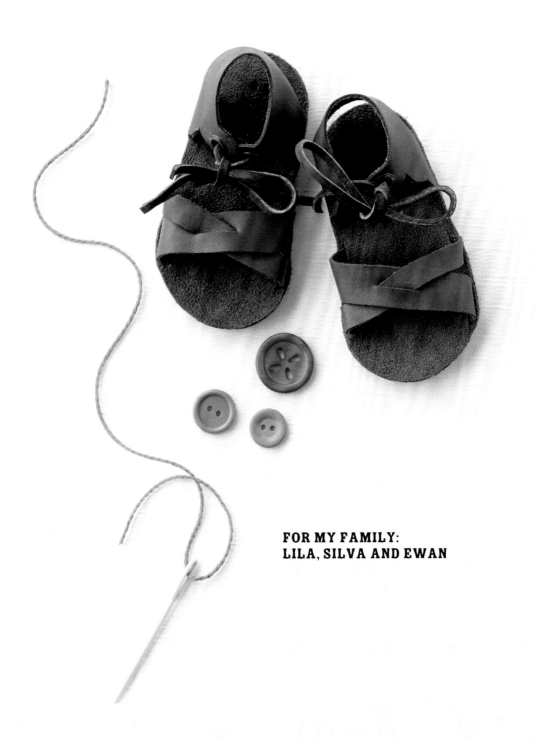

FOR MY FAMILY:
LILA, SILVA AND EWAN

CONTENTS

INTRODUCTION

As a designer, I'm constantly inspired by the world around me and compelled by nature to make things. As a mum of three little ones, I've run the children's lifestyle brand Wild Things for several years now, and continue to develop ideas for clothing and play that stimulate the senses and are full of whimsy and surprise. In this book, my second, I've come up with some beautiful new ideas for clothes for busy children and have also dreamed up some simple things you can make for the home.

I'm from a family of makers and artists, creating things for pleasure but also from necessity. My skills were passed down to me by a family of women who knew instinctively how to dress well. I've been sewing from an early age, whether to create unique gifts or to make something for a big night out… and now making for my three Wild Things.

In this era of mass production, traditional sewing skills have been in decline. The age-old passing down of these techniques skipped a generation, but now tech-savvy creators are keen to soak up new ways to revive artisan skills. With today's instantaneous exchanging of ideas, visual reference is at our fingertips, opening up a world of inspiration and, of course, exciting fabrics to work with.

Colour and pattern are so important to me. Children respond to simple imagery and bold colour, and I create clothes that are easy to wear and don't follow the constraints of the adult world of fashion. Choose fabrics and trims that you and your children love, or upcycle and rework an old garment to make something unique, while creating lasting memories.

The patterns, which are for sizes six months to seven years, are all available online (see page 11), and templates are provided from page 208. These patterns and templates provide you with the starting point for a brand-new and exciting world of shapes and imagery. Many of the projects are adaptable to enable you to interchange elements and create designs that suit your children's own preferences. Some patterns are repeated from my first book, so that if you are new to sewing you can create some of my classic designs.

Whether you are a beginner or an advanced dressmaker, this book is full of projects that you will enjoy making and your children will love. Don't be nervous about having a go – every piece will be unique and something to treasure.

Kirsty xx

GETTING STARTED

POSITIVITY

For new makers starting out, it's important to enjoy the process of creating something, without worrying about the challenges that lie before you. Start with something easy, like an A-line dress. It doesn't matter if you make mistakes – the important thing is not to give up.

I've tried to make each technique simple, and the patterns each have one, two or three buttons to indicate their skill level, from beginner, through moderate, to advanced. For experienced sewers there is plenty here for you to work with. And for maverick makers like me, there is lots of scope for you to add your own touches to the core set of all-round patterns and templates.

SPACE

Setting yourself up with a space to work is key. Even if it has to be mobile to fit around the family, having a place to stash, collect, organise and store your work is important. Often a dining table, or a similar stable surface, is best. The beauty of children's clothes is that they are smaller and easier to manage and so don't require an enormous work surface. Research other crafters' workspaces and organised storage on Pinterest, Instagram or craft magazines for inspiration.

TOOLS OF THE TRADE

Good equipment is important. Scissors that you can actually use are a must. Get to know your sewing machine – study the user manual and make sure you know how to thread it, to adjust the tension and stitch settings and to change a needle. Try out different stitches on a few scraps of fabric or – even better – ask a sewing friend to show you the ropes.

A PERFECT FINISH

Be methodical and take your time to get a good finish. Press seams and prepare as you go along. The projects are written to allow you to make the smaller, more detailed parts first, keeping bigger pieces of fabric folded and ready. That way you can see how the design is coming together. Don't over-handle your fabric, and if you make a mistake simply stop, count to ten, then unpick, press again and carry on. Be patient and don't expect instant results. Remember, perfection is overrated!

CHOICE OF FABRIC

There are endless numbers of lovely online fabric stores, as well as inspirational blogs by talented stitchers offering sewing tutorials. Find a fabric source that stocks the ranges you like or from which you can order haberdashery, such as thread at the same time. Online fabric suppliers offer a fantastic range of cotton-based fabrics, which are easy to sew.

There are two basic types of fabric you can use for making clothes: woven or knitted. Woven fabrics are more stable to work with, especially if you are a beginner. Stretch fabrics, such as jersey, interlock and fleece, require a stitch setting on your sewing machine that will allow the seam to stretch with the garment and not 'crack' (see page 23).

NEW FROM OLD

We've become a generation of gatherers (sometimes hoarders) of eclectic bits and bobs. Simple references to shared memories in clothing are a wonderful way to revive pre-loved fabrics, buttons and trims. Incorporating a simple kept button, or a piece of cloth embroidered by Granny, is a lovely means of bringing nostalgia into a design.

IMPERIAL OR METRIC

Some of us prefer to use the old-school measurements for sewing, so both metric and imperial measurements are given throughout this book. Please use one or the other for accuracy; this is particularly important for quilter's cottons that are sold as 'fat quarters' or quarter-yards, which are cut to give a large quarter of a yard. You can also request a 'skinny quarter', which is cut across the entire width of the fabric. Buying in centimetres, on the other hand, can be a little more flexible, as multiples of 10cm are often sold, giving a little less wastage.

PATTERNS & TEMPLATES

The designs are adaptable but I've provided templates (see page 208) to get you started. We know that some of you prefer to work with traditional patterns, so the patterns are all downloadable online for endless printouts, and can be found here: www.orionbooks.co.uk/wttomakepatterns. You can also find ready-printed patterns for the generic dresses and clothes in my first book, *Wild Things Funky Little Clothes to Sew*.

TIP

To print the patterns, download the pattern file, then save to your computer. Open as a PDF file. Select Print, choosing 'Actual Size' and 'Poster' so that your printer naturally tiles the image for you and prints to scale. Happy sewing!

KIT

- Sewing machine
- Assortment of spare machine needles for use with different fabric weights
- Ironing board and a good-quality steam iron
- Fabric scissors that you find comfortable to use
- Small craft scissors for detailed work
- Seam ripper, useful for unpicking seams
- Dressmaker's pins
- Sewing needles for hand work
- Tailor's chalk or erasable chalk pencil
- Large ruler or pattern-cutting square
- Tape measure

USEFUL TECHNIQUES

APPLIQUÉ

This term comes from the French word for 'to apply'. In sewing it means adding a layer of fabric decoration to a larger piece of fabric. Traditionally, appliqué would have involved intricate handwork using a paper design template and then hand sewing onto the main fabric. A simple alternative is to use a heat-bonding appliqué paper or iron-on, double-sided adhesive web, which is backed with paper on one side.

1. Draw or trace your design onto the paper backing, remembering it will appear in reverse on the right side of the fabric.

2. Cut out each shape.

3. Select a piece of fabric that is slightly larger than your design and heat-press using an iron to bond the design to the wrong side of the fabric, following the manufacturer's instructions.

4. Peel the paper backing from the appliqué fabric and assemble the design onto the main fabric, adhesive side down.

5. Heat-press using an iron to bond the appliqué pieces to the main fabric.

6. Use a sewing machine to stitch 2mm in from the edges of all the pieces. This is known as edge stitching and is quick, easy and effective. After time and washing, the result will be something with a lovely hand-crafted feel. You can also use heavyweight bonding web for a more permanent finish.

BINDING

This is the technique of creating a decorative border to finish an edge, using pre-prepared or self-made fabric. Bias binding is made from bias-cut strips, making it an excellent finish for a curved edge.

1. Cut one strip (or several lengths) of fabric on the bias (at a 45-degree angle to the selvedge). To determine the width of the strips, decide on the depth of the binding (the part visible from the right side), double this, then add seam allowances of 1cm (³/₈in). Heavyweight fabrics require more seam allowance, and lightweight fabrics less. For a plain cotton fabric binding that is 1.5cm (⁵/₈in) deep, 5cm (2in) is a good guide.

2. If necessary, join the ends into one long strip, as for Piping, step 2 (see page 21). Press both long edges in by 1cm (³/₈in).

3. Press the binding in half lengthways.

4. Open out one fold and pin the right side of the binding to the wrong side of the edge you wish to finish, raw edges even. Sew along the opened-out fold line.

5. Press the binding towards the edge along the stitching line and fold it over to the right side of the fabric, with the centre fold even with the raw edge of the fabric and the remaining folded edge just covering the stitching line from step 4. Pin and tack in place, easing the binding as necessary. Stitch slowly close to the edge from the right side, taking care that the binding doesn't twist.

BUTTONHOLES

A basic buttonhole has a bar tack at each end and two sides, which are closely satin stitched. Refer to your sewing machine manual to select the correct setting, and practise on a scrap of similar-weight fabric first. The fabric should be stable and able to take the weight of a heavy satin stitch without clogging. On some lightweight or open-weave fabrics, you may require a small square of interfacing ironed onto the wrong side of the fabric to strengthen it, which is especially important if the button is likely to receive some wear and tear.

1. Mark the top and bottom of the buttonhole along the grain line.

2. Using matching sewing thread, follow the steps shown in your manual to complete the buttonhole in the following order: left side, bottom, right side, top.

3. Using small, sharp scissors or a seam ripper, carefully cut through the centre without snipping through any of the stitching.

BUTTONS

Although there are many styles and sizes of button, there are only two types. One type has two or four central holes through which the stitches are sewn, while the other type has a shank (stem) with a hole running through it.

1. Mark the button position and thread your needle with a double thickness of strong thread.

2. Make backstitches on the front of the garment at the button mark to secure.

3. Bring the needle and thread up through one hole in the button and down through a second hole, or if it has a shank take the needle through the hole in the shank. Repeat several times. If the button has four holes, repeat this step through the second pair of holes.

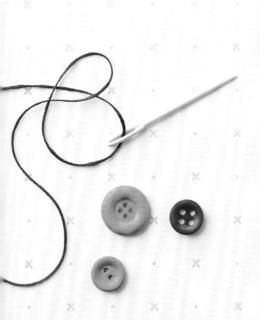

4. If the button doesn't have a shank, you'll need to create a mock shank, so that the button will sit neatly on the buttonhole when fastened. After completing steps 1–3, bring your needle to the front of the garment. You may wish to gently ease the button away from the fabric. Wrap the thread around the stitching several times to create the shank.

5. Take the needle back through to the back of the garment, and sew a few small stitches to secure. Cut the thread.

CUTTING

Choose shears or scissors that are comfortable to hold, especially if you are left-handed, as I am. Use scissors with long blades for cutting fabric, and a smaller pair for fine work or trimming. Always press your fabric before cutting and lay it out on a flat surface.

Arrange the pattern pieces carefully before cutting, to maximise the use of your fabric. The patterns for this book require a seam allowance to be added, so be sure to leave enough room between the pieces. If there is a pile, nap or print direction, make sure that the pattern pieces are running in the same direction.

Pin each pattern piece to the fabric, lining up any grain lines on the pattern with the lengthwise grain of the fabric, and placing any fold lines on the pattern against the fold of a double layer of fabric. Mark around the pattern piece with an erasable marker such as tailor's chalk on the reverse of the fabric, adding seam allowances as necessary. Cut the fabric on a flat surface, without lifting it up.

EASING

Easing involves gently enabling one longer seam to match another, usually when sewing curved or gathered edges. Start by matching both pieces of fabric at the ends or between notches. Pin at 45 degrees to the edge, distributing the excess fabric evenly and using enough pins to keep the fabric layers flat. Ease the two layers as you sew them together so that the seam line is smooth.

FRENCH SEAM

This is a seam that is first sewn with wrong sides of fabric together, then trimmed and pressed, and then the process is repeated with the right sides together, so that the raw edges are enclosed with the seam. It makes an ideal alternative finish for fine fabrics, in which you may see the seam inside and don't want to see overlocking.

GATHERING

This can be used to add fullness or detail to clothing. If you are cutting fabric to be gathered, such as for a simple skirt, a good rule of thumb is to double the width of your fabric.

1. Set your machine to the longest straight stitch setting. With the fabric right side up, stitch one thread's width inside the seam line, leaving lengths of loose thread at each end.

2. Stitch in the same way 5mm (¼in) from the first stitching, within the seam allowance.

3. Turn the fabric so it is wrong side up. At one end of the two lines of stitching, wrap the two ends of the bobbin threads in a figure-of-eight around a pin.

TIP
A quick alternative way to gather fabric is to stitch 5mm- (¼in-) wide elastic just inside the seam line on the wrong side of the fabric, gently stretching the elastic as you stitch to create a soft gather.

4. At the other end, very gently pull the two bobbin threads to gather up the fabric, carefully easing the gathers along the stitching as you go. When the gathered edge is the desired length, fasten the thread ends.

HEMS

Hems are used to finish the lower raw edge of a garment. Normally a hem will be turned under once, then a second time to conceal any raw edges. Hems can be stitched into place by machine, or by hand using a slipstitch or other hand hemming stitch.

INVISIBLE ZIP

An invisible zip is often used on dresses where a professional finish is required, for example at a waistline, because the zipper teeth and the stitching are not visible. You need a special invisible zip for this. You can use an ordinary machine zipper foot, but an invisible-zip foot makes it easier.

1. Overlock all seams if the garment is unlined. Using tailor's chalk, mark the position of the invisible zip along the seam line on the right side of both the left-hand and the right-hand fabric pieces.

2. Open the zip and, using a cool iron, press the rolled zip teeth back slightly.

3. Fit the zipper foot on your machine and adjust it to allow the stitching to sit as close as possible to the zip teeth.

4. Place one tape of the open zip on one fabric piece, with right sides together and the teeth running along the seam line. The entire tape should be within the seam allowance. Pin and, if you wish, tack in place.

5. With the needle positioned correctly for the zipper foot, stitch the tape in place 2mm from the teeth, rolling the teeth flat as you sew. When you reach the marked end, backstitch to secure. Remove the tacking if used.

6. Move the needle to the other side of the zipper foot. With the two fabric pieces side by side and right side up, flip the stitched piece over so it is on top of the unstitched piece, and fold it back out of the way. Pin, tack if you wish, and stitch the remaining tape to the bottom fabric piece in the same way as in steps 4 and 5.

7. Change to a standard machine foot and close the zip. Stitch the seam below the zip in the usual way (see page 24), but start at the bottom of the seam and sew to the marked point by the zip, pushing the unstitched part of the tapes out of the way. Backstitch to secure.

OVERLOCKING

This is a good way to finish the raw edges of fabric, though a zigzag stitch on a standard sewing machine will suffice. Alternatively, a French seam or bound seam can be used instead. Fully lined garments need not be overlocked. Follow the instructions in your machine manual to overlock raw edges.

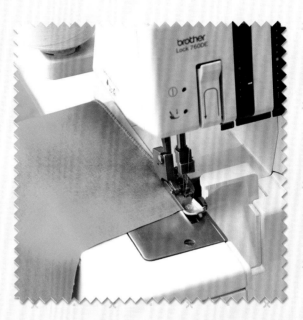

NOTCHES

A notch is a mark on a pattern piece that denotes where it, and a corresponding notch on another pattern piece, are intended to be placed together. Transfer notches from the pattern to the fabric, and make a small nick within the seam allowance when you cut out the fabric to transfer the notch to all the pieces.

PILE & NAP

The raised pile on a fabric such as velvet or corduroy lies in a clear direction. This means you need to cut everything with the pile running in the same direction (generally running down the fabric) and you may need to allow extra fabric to do so. On napped fabrics, such as flannel, the surface has been brushed to create a fuzzy effect, so they are treated in the same way as pile fabrics.

PIPING

A method of adding detail to seams or edges, piping is a lovely feature on children's clothing, and it allows you to add bold highlight colours to plain or print fabrics. Cotton piping cord can be inserted to give a round effect and rigidity to the piping but is not essential.

1. Cut strips of fabric on the bias (at a 45-degree angle to the selvedge) – the width of the strips should be double the exposed width, plus two seam allowances, plus enough to cover the cording if used. For example, for 5mm (¼in) piping made with a 1cm (³⁄₈in) seam allowance, strips 3cm (1¼in) wide should be sufficient.

2. You may need to join the strips together at the ends to make the piping long enough. To do this, first cut each end at a 45-degree angle, and mark 5mm (¼in) seam allowances. Now pin two ends with right sides together, with the marked seam lines aligning. Stitch and then press the seam open.

3. Press the strip in half lengthways, wrong sides together. If you are not using cord inside the piping, skip the next step.

4. If you are using cord inside the piping, fit the zipper foot or piping foot on your machine. Using the pattern piece as a guide, cut the piping cord to the required length, less 5mm (¼in) at each end. Place it inside the pressed strip, with the ends 5mm (¼in) from the ends of the strip. Pin close to the cord, with the raw edges of the strip even, then stitch close to the cord.

5. To pipe a seam, place the piping on the right side of one fabric piece, with the seam lines even (you may wish to mark these first) and with the fold of the piping facing inwards.

6. Stitch along the seam line. Now place the other fabric piece on top, right side down, with the raw edges even with the first fabric piece. Pin and then stitch along the seam line.

PRESSING

Use a good-quality steam iron and a clean ironing-board cover. Alternatively, have a pressing cloth to hand to keep things clean and protected. Pressing seams open or to one side is essential to achieve a good finish, and you should do this as you go along. Generally press on the reverse to protect the fabric. Prevent a pile from flattening by pressing the piece face down on a scrap of the same fabric.

ROULEAU LOOP

This is made from bias-cut fabric and used to loop around a button to form a fastening. Cut an 8 × 3cm (3 × 1¼in) strip of fabric on the bias. Fold it lengthways, right sides together, and stitch along one edge, leaving a long length of thread at the end. Carefully thread this end through a darning needle, feed the needle back through the channel, and pull the fabric through to form the rouleau.

SEAM

A plain seam is achieved by placing two pieces of fabric right sides together and sewing a straight line of stitching the required distance from the raw edge. The fabric from the seam line to the raw edge is called the seam allowance. In this book all the seam allowances are 1cm (³⁄₈in) unless otherwise specified. Other seam finishes such as French seams (see page 17) can also be used.

SNIPPING CURVED EDGES & CORNERS

Curved seams, for example at armholes and necklines, need to be carefully snipped within the seam allowance – not too close to the stitching – so that, when turned through, the edge remains curved and lies flat. Corners should be trimmed by snipping across them at a 45-degree angle to reduce bulk when turned through.

STRETCH FABRIC

For garments made from stretch fabric, the seams need to be stitched differently to prevent them from 'cracking' when the garments are worn. Most contemporary sewing machines have a variety of settings, including zigzag, mock-overlock and sometimes twin-needle settings, so refer to your machine manual. A simple way to create stretch seams is to stitch along the seam lines using a narrow zigzag stitch. To finish the raw edges, either overlock them or stitch them using a wider, looser zigzag stitch.

TACKING

Temporarily securing layers with long stitches is called tacking, or basting, and helps with precision and fine work. It is usually done by hand but machine tacking is also possible. Tacking threads are removed after sewing.

To hand tack, sew close to the seam line but within the seam allowance, using stitches about 5mm (¼in) long and between 5mm (¼in) and 3cm (1¼in) apart.

To machine tack, set your machine to the longest straight stitch and stitch just inside the seam line.

TOPSTITCHING

This can be used for decorative purposes but more often it is used to achieve a flat, strong edge finish, for example on a collar, cuff or patch pocket. It simply means stitching through one or more layers from the right side of the garment. Because it may be impossible to see the seam guidelines on your sewing machine needle plate, you can keep the topstitching parallel to the edge by using the machine foot as a guide for 5mm (¼in) stitching; for wider widths, a row of tacking or a strip of masking tape can be used to keep the stitching parallel.

ZIP

Zips can be applied in various ways (for invisible zips, see page 19), but the following is a guide to inserting a standard nylon zip using the centred-application method, which is ideal for necklines.

1. Overlock all seams if the garment is unlined. Mark the length of the zip along the opening from the top of the neckline downwards. Sew a seam up to this point.

2. Press the seam open and continue to press it open right to the top. If you wish, you can machine tack this portion of the seam before pressing it open, but it isn't essential.

3. Pin the zip into position, face down on the wrong side of the fabric pieces, centring the teeth over the opening, and then hand tack in place and remove the pins. The aim is for the zip teeth to be covered by fabric.

4. Referring to your machine manual, select the correct setting and foot for your machine. A zipper foot allows you to sew closer to the teeth, so move the needle to the correct side of the foot. Working from the right side, stitch the zip in place an appropriate distance from the edge – about 5mm (¼in) – depending on the weight of the fabric and the width of your seam allowance. Pivot the fabric at the corners. Make sure the distance from the centre is the same on both sides of the zip and the stitching is parallel to the opening. Be careful not to stitch through the teeth at the bottom. Remove any tacking.

5. Either hand stitch the facing into place around the zip, or carefully machine stitch it into place by sewing over the original stitches, but this time through all the layers.

MEASURING YOUR CHILD

I have provided clothing sizes below, as guidelines, which are useful if your child isn't to hand. Measure your child's waist, chest and height to select the appropriate pattern size. The dress projects also include a guide for you to work out your required fabric lengths. For US quarter measurements, request thin quarters and not fat quarters to be cut from the bolt, so the fabric is cut as one continual length.

AVERAGE MEASUREMENTS BY AGE*

AGE	HEIGHT	CHEST	WAIST
6–18 months	to 80cm (31½in)	to 50cm (20in)	to 46cm (18in)
18 months–3 years	to 98cm (39in)	to 54cm (21in)	to 50cm (20in)
3–5 years	to 110cm (44in)	to 58cm (23in)	to 54cm (21in)
5–7 years	to 122cm (48in)	to 63cm (25in)	to 58cm (23in)

*If the child you are creating the garment for is smaller or larger than average, you will need to adjust to fit.

A-LINE DRESS (SEE PAGE 30): FINISHED MEASUREMENTS

SIZE	LENGTH FROM SNP*	CHEST	HEM CIRCUMFERENCE
6–18 months	44cm (17½in)	55cm (22in)	80cm (31½in)
18 months–3 years	49cm (19½in)	60cm (24in)	90cm (35½in)
3–5 years	55cm (22in)	66cm (26in)	100cm (39½in)
5–7 years	62cm (24½in)	71cm (28in)	110cm (44in)

*SNP – side neck point (measured from point on garment closest to neck)

CHARACTER DRESS (SEE PAGE 94): FINISHED MEASUREMENTS

SIZE	LENGTH FROM SNP*	CHEST
6–18 months	44cm (17½in)	58cm (23in)
18 months–3 years	49cm (19½in)	62cm (24½in)
3–5 years	55cm (22in)	68cm (27in)
5–7 years	62cm (24½in)	75cm (30in)

*SNP – side neck point (measured from point on garment closest to neck)

DUNGAREES (SEE PAGE 110): FINISHED MEASUREMENTS

SIZE	LENGTH*	HIP	HEIGHT OF CHILD
6–18 months	45cm (18in)	68cm (27in)	to 80cm (31½in)
18 months–3 years	61cm (24in)	76cm (30in)	to 98cm (39in)
3–5 years	75cm (30in)	84cm (33in)	to 110cm (44in)

*From underarm to hem extended

DRESSES & ROMPERS

CHIC A-LINE DRESS
WITH CAP SLEEVES

This smart little dress is so grown-up and chic. It is suitable for most fabrics but perfect in a large-scale Scandinavian-style print. Making the length shorter would create a real sixties feel. It has a little cap sleeve but could easily be made without.

YOU WILL NEED

A-line dress and cap sleeve patterns (follow the lines for a seamed shoulder)

1 length of dress fabric (see Calculating fabric lengths, below)

1 length of lining fabric (optional) (see Calculating fabric lengths, below)

Plain cotton for facings (optional)

Contrast fabric for pockets, if desired

18cm (7in) matching zip (for Option B)

1 button (for Option A)

Matching sewing thread

Tailor's chalk

CUTTING OUT

Before you start, decide whether your dress will be fully lined or will have a simple faced neck and armholes, depending on the weight of your fabric or the desired weight of the dress. You can also choose to have a simple keyhole opening (Option A) or a zip fastening at the back neck (Option B).

NOTE: Seam allowances are 1cm (3/8in) unless otherwise specified.

(CON'T)

CALCULATING FABRIC LENGTHS	6 MONTHS-3 YEARS	3-5 YEARS
Width 110cm (44in) lined dress *	70cm (27½in)	80cm (31½in)
Width 150cm (60in) lined dress *	70cm (27½in)	80cm (31½in)
Width 110cm (44in) dress with facing	1m (39in)	120cm (47in)
Width 150cm (60in) dress with facing	1m (39in)	120cm (47in)

* For the lined dress you will need the same amount of lining fabric.

1. Choose the best size for your child, using the guide on page 26. Trace the pattern for the A-line dress and sleeve available online (see page 11), following the lines for the correct size. Make a pattern for the front, with the neck sitting lower, and another full pattern for the back. Make a pattern for the cap sleeve. You will notice the pattern front and back are marked with single and double notches so that you can position each sleeve correctly. Cut out two pairs of sleeves. As the sleeve is a small, simple cap sleeve, then it makes good sense to line it to create a good finish to the curved edge, regardless of whether the dress itself is lined.

2. Press the fabric and arrange it on a flat surface so you can cut out one whole dress front and two separate back half pieces. Make sure the centre front and the grain line on each back piece are parallel to the selvedge. If you have a large print fabric and would like to cut the back as one piece then you can do this, but you will need to follow instructions for a keyhole back dress (see page 34). Choosing this option requires the armholes to be overlocked and turned back, as the whole dress cannot be bagged out or turned through without a centre back seam.

3. Mark around the pattern pieces using tailor's chalk, adding 1cm (³⁄₈in) all around for seam allowances, and 2cm (³⁄₄in) at the hem. Cut out the pieces carefully.

4. To make the dress with facings to finish the neck edge and armholes, cut facing patterns by drawing a straight line across the body patterns (as marked), 4cm (1¹⁄₂in) below the armholes. The facings can be in the same fabric as the main dress or in a plain cotton.

5. To make a fully lined dress, you will need to cut a complete new dress from lining fabric. The lining dress should be at least 2cm (³⁄₄in) shorter.

POCKET (OPTIONAL)

1. Using the pattern provided, cut the pocket from matching or contrast fabric, and overlock the edges. Overlocking is not essential but prevents the pockets from fraying on the inside. Press the curved edges under by 1cm (³⁄₈in).

2. Fold under the top edge of the pocket twice by 1cm (³⁄₈in) and press. Topstitch to secure.

3. Pin the pocket in position on the dress front. Topstitch around the side and bottom edges, backstitching at the start and finish.

SLEEVES

1. You will have two pairs of sleeves, one in the main fabric, one in the lining.

2. Place each pair – outer (main fabric) and inner (lining fabric) – right sides together, and stitch along the outer curved edge of each sleeve, 1 cm (⅜in) from the edge.

3. Press the seam open and then fold into place and press again. Sew the lining to the main fabric, wrong sides together, along the edge that will adjoin the body.

JOINING

1. Pin the dress front to the back pieces at the shoulders, right sides together, and sew the shoulder seams. Press the seams open. Repeat for the facings (or lining).

2. Pin the sleeves in position around the armholes of the dress, right sides together, matching notches. Sew in place.

3. Place the facing (or lining) on the dress, right sides together. Pin around the neckline; stitch. Pin the facing (or lining) around each armhole; stitch, taking care not to catch the sleeve in the seam – it may help to roll the sleeve a little so it doesn't get in the way. Snip into the curved seam allowances around the neckline and the armholes, leaving the back open to add either a keyhole back (Option A on page 34) or a zip (Option B on page 34).

4. Turn the dress through and carefully press.

5. Overlock all the remaining raw edges.

(CON'T)

1. Mark the length of the back neck opening from the neckline down the centre back of the dress – about 8cm (3¼in). Pin the back pieces right sides together and sew a seam from the hemline to this point. Press the seam open and continue to press up to the neck. Repeat for the facing (or lining).

2. Prepare a rouleau loop from the main fabric (see page 22). Pin the folded loop in position at the neck opening. The loop should be large enough to comfortably fit around your button plus 2cm (¾ in). Finish the neck opening by pinning the dress and facing (or lining) together and then stitching all the way around the neckline.

3. To finish the armholes, carefully sew the dress and facing (or lining) together, with the cap sleeve trapped inside between both layers. Trim the seams carefully to release the curve.

4. Turn the dress through to the right side and gently press the edges.

5. Pin the side seams, right sides of the dress and right side of the facing (or lining) together, carefully matching the armhole seams. Sew, overlock (if required) and press.

1. Pin the two main-fabric back pieces along the centre back edges, right sides together. Mark the length of your zip along the opening from the top of the neckline downwards. If you are using a plain zip, sew a seam from the bottom of the dress up to this point, and follow instructions on page 24 to insert the zip.

2. If you are using an invisible zip then the zip will first be sewn into place to the left and right halves of the dress before sewing the centre back seam. See page 19 for more instructions on how to insert an invisible zip.

3. Press the seam open and continue to press the seam allowances open all the way to the top.

4. Insert the zip (see page 24).

5. Repeat steps 3, 4 and 5 for Option A (above).

6. Slipstitch the lining into place along the zip edge on the inside.

TIP
For added detail, do the topstitching in a bright contrast thread or use a fun, decorative button.

FINISHING

1. Finish the hem edge by turning 1 cm (³⁄₈in) under twice and stitching down. You can stitch the hem by hand if you prefer.

2. If desired, topstitch around the neck edge and topstitch the underarms to the sleeves, 5mm (¼in) from the edges, taking care around the curves. This will give a neat finish.

3. If you chose Option A, sew a button into place (see page 16).

OUT AT SEA DRESS

This beautiful dress has a lovely grown-up feel because of its narrow self-fabric belt, and so is suitable for older girls. The classic A-line is given added interest with the soft tucks at the neck. Made here in sky blue linen and lined with soft cotton, it is trimmed with colourful origami sailboats, giving it a real feel of seaside holidays. To keep it simple, there is no topstitching, as linen can be worked and pressed beautifully without needing it.

YOU WILL NEED

A-line dress pattern (follow the lines for a seamed shoulder, and with a tuck at the neckline as desired)

Boat and sun templates

1 length of dress fabric (see Calculating fabric lengths, below)

1 length of lining fabric (optional) (see Calculating fabric lengths, below)

Plain cotton for facings (optional)

Contrast fabric for boats

12.5cm (5in) strip of fabric, cut from the full width of the fabric for the hem trim

Iron-on double-sided adhesive web

1 button

Matching sewing thread

Tailor's chalk

CUTTING OUT

This dress is sleeveless. Before you start, decide whether it will be fully lined or will have a simple faced neck and armholes.

NOTE: Seam allowances are 1cm (³⁄₈in) unless otherwise specified.

(CON'T)

CALCULATING FABRIC LENGTHS	6 MONTHS-3 YEARS	3-5 YEARS
Width 110cm (44in) lined dress *	70cm (27½in)	80cm (31½in)
Width 150cm (60in) lined dress *	70cm (27½in)	80cm (31½in)
Width 110cm (44in) dress with facing	1m (39in)	120cm (47in)
Width 150cm (60in) dress with facing	1m (39in)	120cm (47in)

* For the lined dress you will need the same amount of lining fabric.

1. Choose the best size for your child, using the guide on page 26. Trace the pattern for the A-line dress available online (see page 11), following the lines for the correct size (with or without the front neck tuck if you like). Follow the line above the true hemline as the added contrast band of the sea fabric added to the hem will make the finished length. Make a pattern for the front, with the neck sitting lower, and another full pattern for the back.

2. Press the fabric and arrange it on a flat surface so you can cut out one dress front and one back. Make sure the centre front and the centre back are parallel to the selvedge. If you are using a print fabric, take care that the direction of the pattern is the same for each piece.

3. Mark around the pattern pieces using tailor's chalk, adding 1cm (3/8in) all around for seam allowances, and 2cm (3/4in) at the hem. Cut out the pieces carefully.

4. To make the dress with facings to finish the neck edge and armholes, cut facing patterns by drawing a straight line across the body patterns (as marked), 4cm (1 1/2in) below the armholes. The facings can be in the same fabric as the main dress or in a plain cotton.

5. To make a fully lined dress, you will need to cut a complete new dress from lining fabric. The lining dress should be at least 2cm (3/4in) shorter.

ADDING DETAIL TO FRONT

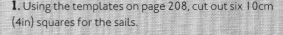

1. Using the templates on page 208, cut out six 10cm (4in) squares for the sails.

2. Press each sail in half, wrong sides together, then fold the corners towards the raw edge so they meet in the middle, and press again.

3. Following the instructions on page 13, back the boat fabrics with iron-on double-sided adhesive web. Using the template on page 208, trace the boat shape onto the backing paper. Remove the backing paper.

4. Space the boats evenly in a row along the front and back hem, 1cm (3/8in) from the raw edge.

5. Catching the folded raw edge of the sails under the boats, press into place to bond to the dress. Topstitch all around.

6. Pin the four soft tucks at the front neckline, so that two are facing left and two are facing right, spacing them evenly at the centre front. Check the pinned neckline against the pattern for the facing to make sure the size is correct. Stitch in place a fraction less than 1cm (³⁄₈in) from the edge.

BELT

To make the belt, cut a 4 × 100cm (1½ × 40in) strip of fabric. Press under 1cm (³⁄₈in) on all four edges, then press in half lengthways. Stitch close to the long edge.

FINISHING THE NECKLINE

1. Pin the front facing (or lining) to the front piece, right sides together. Sew around the armholes and neckline. Trim the curved edges within the seam allowance to release the curve then turn through carefully and press.

2. Pin the back facing (or lining) to the back piece, right sides together, and mark the position of the keyhole opening with tailor's chalk.

3. Mark the stitching line for the keyhole opening, to create a neat symmetrical curve at the bottom end when turned through.

4. Prepare three rouleau loops from the main fabric (see page 22). Pin one of the folded loops in position at the marked keyhole opening, so that the loop is sandwiched between the back and the back facing (or lining). The back neck loop should be large enough to comfortably fit around your button, plus seam allowance. (The other two loops will be used as belt loops – see Joining, step 2.)

5. Sew around the armholes and neckline as for the front (see step 1), following the marked stitching line to create the keyhole shape.

6. Cut down the centre back to create the keyhole opening, and trim the edges. Turn through carefully and press.

(CON'T)

JOINING

1. Pin the turned-through dress front and back together, right sides of main fabric together, matching shoulder seams so all four shoulder edges meet, as shown. Sew the four layers together 1 cm (³⁄₈in) from the edge at each shoulder point.

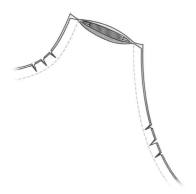

2. Pin a folded loop to each side seam at the waistline notch to create belt loops; stitch in place.

3. Pin the side seams, with the right sides of the dress and right side of the facing (or lining) together, carefully matching the armhole seams. Sew in a continuous seam on each side, and press. Overlock the raw edges.

4. Turn the dress through, press again and topstitch around the neck and armholes if required, 1 cm (³⁄₈in) from the edge.

FINISHING

1. Press the long strip in half lengthways, wrong sides together, and cut it to the same length as the distance around the lower edge of the dress, plus 1 cm (³⁄₈in) seam allowance at each end. Pin the folded ends to each other, right sides together, and stitch to create a continuous folded contrast band. Press the seam open, but do not turn it through.

2. Pin the double-thickness band to the lower edge of the dress, right sides together and raw edges even, matching the stitched end of the strip to one side seam on the dress. Stitch all the way around. Overlock the raw edges, and press the double-thickness band away from the dress. Topstitch close to the seam.

3. Sew a button into place at the neck opening.

4. Overlock and hem the facing (or lining) by turning back 1 cm (³⁄₈in), and press.

FOXY POCKET DRESS

Unlined and using the simple A-line block, this modern pinafore has a hidden pocket that is perfect for little girls at play. The style is perfect for woven and jersey fabrics, especially fleece. Use funky bright geometric patterns for contrast, and try creating different faces and ears. What's more, there's a cute little twist to the back of the dress, which has a simple triangular fox tail.

YOU WILL NEED

A-line dress pattern (follow the lines for a seamed shoulder)

Fox face templates

1 length of dress fabric (see Calculating fabric lengths, below)

1 fat quarter of contrast fabric for inner pockets

Funky fabric scraps for ears and tail, about 30cm (12in) square

Plain contrast fabric scraps in two colours for nose and snout

Iron-on double-sided adhesive web

1m (39in) bias binding

2 contrast buttons for eyes

1 button for neck opening

Bright contrast sewing thread

Tailor's chalk

CUTTING OUT

This dress is bound at the neckline and armholes, with a simple faced keyhole opening at the back.

NOTE: Seam allowances are 1cm (³⁄₈in) unless otherwise specified.

1. Choose the best size for your child, using the guide on page 26. Trace the pattern for the A-line dress available online (see page 11), following the lines for the correct size and observing the horizontal line marked Foxy Pocket Dress. Make patterns for the upper front, lower front, upper back and lower back, facings and pocket.

(CON'T)

CALCULATING FABRIC LENGTHS	6 MONTHS-3 YEARS	3-5 YEARS
Width 110cm (44in) dress	70cm (27½in)	1m (39in)
Width 150cm (60in) dress	70cm (27½in)	1m (39in)

2. Press the fabric and arrange it on a flat surface so you can cut out each piece. Make sure the centre front and the centre back are parallel to the selvedge.

3. Mark around the pattern pieces using tailor's chalk, adding 1 cm (³⁄₈in) all around for seam allowances, and 2 cm (¾in) at the hem. Cut out the pieces carefully.

4. For the facing, cut a U-shaped piece of fabric.

5. Cut two pockets from the contrast plain fabric. Before you begin to assemble, overlock the edges of all main pieces and pocket bags to finish.

POCKET & TAIL

This requires some tricky sewing.

1. Using the pattern available online (see page 11), cut out four ears: two in funky fabric for the ear fronts and two in plain fabric for the ear backs.

2. To prepare each ear, pin each ear front to an ear back, right sides together, and sew along two sides, 5 mm (¼in) from the edge. Trim off the corners of the seam allowance (see page 23). Turn through and press from the plain side. Topstitch close to the edges.

3. For the oval nose, bond adhesive web to the wrong side of a scrap of contrast fabric (see page 13). Using the pattern, cut out the nose.

4. Assemble the face onto the lower dress portion. For the triangular snout, use the pattern, adding 1 cm (³⁄₈in) all around, to cut out the snout. Press under 1 cm (³⁄₈in) on two edges. Pin the snout to the lower portion of the dress at the centre, as marked. Topstitch in place.

5. Peel off the backing paper from the oval nose and position on the pocket at the bottom of the snout, overlapping the point; cover with a cloth and iron in place (see page 13). Topstitch around the edge – if you find this difficult, simply stitch horizontally and then vertically, creating a cross shape.

6. Assemble the ears onto the upper dress portion. Pin the ears in place as marked, on either side of the snout, with raw edges even. Stitch in place slightly less than 1cm (³⁄₈in) from the edge.

7. To join the underside pocket bag to the top half of the dress sew into place between the marked notches, as above, with right sides facing, trapping the ears as you sew. Repeat to add the underside pocket bag.

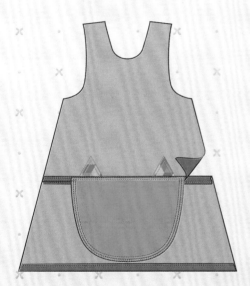

8. Using the pattern, cut out two tails: one in funky fabric for the tail front and one in plain fabric for the tail back. Sew as you had for the ears (see Pocket & tail, step 2).

JOINING

1. Pin the upper front to the lower front, right sides together, along the seam and the pocket bag edges. Sew up to the pocket-opening point on both sides and continue along the pocket bag edges.

2. Position the pieces where the pocket will sit. Pin the pocket bag layers together through the dress. Using tailor's chalk, mark the pocket curve on the right side of the dress. With the right side of the dress front on top, topstitch the pocket in place through all three layers, with two parallel lines of stitching using a contrast thread.

3. To add contrast and to secure, topstitch the pocket opening 5mm (¼in) from the edge. Repeat by topstitching along the seam that joins the top and bottom dress pieces.

4. Pin the upper back to the lower back, right sides together, trapping the raw edge of the tail triangle in the seam. Press the seam open and topstitch along it in the same way, as above.

FACING & BINDING EDGES

1. Place the facing on the top edge of the dress, right sides together. Pin around the neckline; stitch. Mark the length of the back neck opening from the neckline down the centre back of the dress – about 8cm (3¼in). Pin around this mark and carefully cut down the line.

2. Using a short stitch length, sew 5mm (¼in) from the line, and gently curve inwards to the point where the drawn line ends. With the machine needle still in the fabric, release the machine foot, and pivot the fabric 180 degrees to sew back along the opposite side of the opening. Carefully turn back and press.

3. Following the instructions for Binding on page 14, cut a 4cm- (1½-) wide bias strip of contrast print fabric to finish the neck edge; it should be the length of the neckline plus an added 8cm (3¼in) to create a loop for your fastening.

4. Unfold the binding and pin the right side to the inside of the neckline. Sew in place 5mm (¼in) from the edge. Press back carefully, and fold the binding round to the front face of the garment. Pin, then stitch 1mm from the edge, trimming and turning back the starting end to conceal the raw edge. At the opposite end continue to sew the remaining part of the strip. Fold this into a loop and sew into place.

5. Cut two more bias strips, each as long as the distance around the armhole, and bind the armholes (see page 14).

6. Pin the side seams, right sides of the dress and right side of the facing together, carefully matching the armhole seams. Sew and press.

FINISHING

1. Finish the hem edge by turning 1cm (⅜in) under twice and stitching down, using contrast thread.

2. Sew the button eyes in place on the pocket.

3. Sew the back neck button into place.

CONTRARY MARY PINAFORE

'Mary, Mary, quite contrary, how does your garden grow?' Very well, it seems, on this cheerful and colourful toddler's dress, which is sure to put a smile on everyone's face. The appliqué is simple and bold, with a lovely tactile quality. Made here in soft cotton corduroy, it would also look fantastic in denim, a summery floral fabric or a geometric print.

YOU WILL NEED

A-line dress pattern (follow the lines marked for a button shoulder fastening)

Flower templates

1 length of dress fabric (see Calculating fabric lengths, below)

30cm (12in) square of yellow or orange fabric for flower centre

Contrast fabric (plain or patterned) for flower petals, stem and leaves

30cm (12in) square of iron-on double-sided adhesive web

2 chunky buttons, about 2.5cm (1in) in diameter

Matching contrast sewing thread (optional)

Tailor's chalk

CUTTING OUT

This unlined dress is sleeveless, with buttoned shoulders.

NOTE: Seam allowances are 1cm (³⁄₈in) unless otherwise specified.

1. Choose the best size for your child, using the guide on page 26. Trace the pattern for the A-line dress available online (see page 11), following the lines for the correct size. Make a pattern for the front, with the neck sitting lower, and another for the back.

(CON'T)

CALCULATING FABRIC LENGTHS	6 MONTHS-3 YEARS	3-5 YEARS
Width 110cm (44in) dress	1m (39in)	120cm (47in)
Width 150cm (60in) dress	1m (39in)	120cm (47in)

2. Press the fabric and arrange it on a flat surface so you can cut out one dress front, one back and matching facings. Make sure the centre front and centre back are parallel to the selvedge.

3. Mark around the pattern pieces using tailor's chalk, adding 1cm (³⁄₈in) all around for seam allowances, and 2cm (³⁄₄in) at the hem. Cut out the pieces carefully. Cut a front and back facing to the line marked on the pattern by drawing a straight line across the body patterns (as marked).

APPLIQUÉ FLOWER

1. Iron adhesive web to the wrong side of the contrast fabric for the flower centre, stem and leaves (see page 13). On the reverse paper side of the web-backed fabric, draw around the templates on page 208 and cut out one centre, one stem and two leaves.

2. For the petals, choose bright contrasting colours. Bond adhesive web to the wrong side of a scrap of contrast fabric (see page 13). Using the template on page 208, cut out the petals.

3. Mark the flower position on the dress front using tailor's chalk, and arrange the petals in position around it.

4. Remove the paper backing from the petals. Place them in position, adhesive side down, and press to bond (see page 13).

5. Stitch around the edges of the flower centre, stem and leaves, using matching or contrast sewing thread.

6. Repeat the steps above for the flower centre, the stem and the two leaves. Sew a line through the centre of each of the leaves.

JOINING

1. Pin the dress front to the back, right sides together, at one side seam. Stitch the seam, overlock and then press open. Open out the dress front and back, and place it flat on your work surface, right side up.

2. Pin the facing front to the back, right sides together, at the same side seam as for the dress. Stitch the seam, overlock, and then press open. Finish the lower edge either by turning it under twice by 5mm (¼in) and then stitching, or by overlocking.

3. Place the facing on the dress, right sides together, and pin around the neck and armholes and across the shoulders. Sew 5mm (¼in) from the edge. Snip into the curved seam allowances and across the corners, taking care not to cut through the stitching itself.

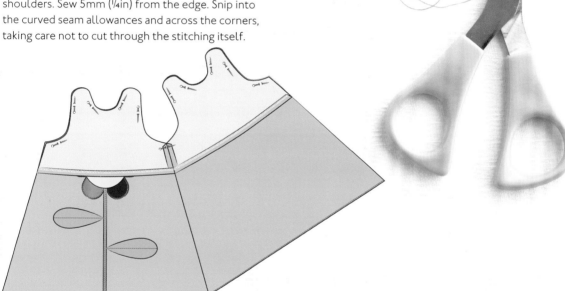

4. Pin the front to the back of the dress and facing at the remaining side seam, and sew in one continuous seam. Overlock and press.

5. Turn the dress through, rolling the fabric gently in places to shape the curved edges. Press, then topstitch 5mm (¼in) from the edge around the armholes and neckline.

FINISHING

1. Hem the dress by turning under the bottom edge twice by 1cm (⅜in) and then stitching.

2. Mark the position of the buttonholes on the back and then stitch (see page 15). Sew the buttons in position on the front.

BALLOON PARTY DRESS

With its fuller skirt, this classic design is a perfect starting point for little girls who love dancing, and the sash makes the dress ideal for parties. Most fabrics are suitable for the dress, but plain cottons are easy to source in a range of bright shades, and the balloons can be made using colourful scraps. For added drama, a pettiskirt can be worn under the dress.

YOU WILL NEED

Party dress pattern

Balloon templates

1m (39in) fabric for the dress: this will provide adequate fabric for the gathered skirt and the bodice.

1m (39in) fabric for the lining

Contrast fabric for the piping (optional)

Coloured fabrics for the balloons

10cm (4in) strip of contrast fabric, cut from the full width of the fabric, for the sash

Scraps of mixed fabrics for the rainbow bunting hem (optional)

Iron-on, double-sided adhesive bonding web

Narrow ribbon or tape for the balloon strings

Coloured ribbons for the balloon ties (optional)

Matching invisible or plain zip, 30cm (12in) or 36cm (14in), depending on dress size

Matching sewing thread

Tailor's chalk

Note:
If you are using a border print which runs along the selvedge of the skirt, allow about 75cm (30in) if the border is at both edges, or 150cm (60in) if not.

CUTTING OUT

This lined dress is sleeveless and has a zip fastening at the back neck. The skirt is gathered onto the bodice.

NOTE: Seam allowances are 1cm (³⁄₈in) unless otherwise specified.

1. Decide how long you want the skirt, and add 4cm (1½in) for the waist seam allowance and the hem. Fold the fabric in half so that the selvedges meet. Cut the skirt to the required length across the full width of the fabric.

(CON'T)

2. Because the dress is lined, you will need to cut a new skirt from lining fabric. The lining skirt should be at least 2.5cm (1in) shorter.

3. Choose the best size for your child, using the guide on page 26. Trace the pattern for the party dress bodice, following the lines for the correct size. Make a pattern for the bodice front and another for the bodice back. Cut out one bodice front and two bodice back pieces.

4. Cut out the same bodice pieces from lining fabric.

> **TIP**
> This dress could also be made without the appliqué or with a different trim, such as the Out At Sea Dress (see page 36). You could also add a cap sleeve (see page 33).

BODICE & CONTRAST PIPING (OPTIONAL)

1. Pin the main-fabric bodice front to the main-fabric bodice back pieces at the shoulders, right sides together. Stitch the shoulder seams and press open. Repeat for the lining.

2. You are now ready to add piping to the neckline and armhole edges if desired. To create a 5mm (¼in) piping, cut bias strips of fabric long enough to add to each edge, and 3cm (1¼in) in width.

3. Pin then sew each edging into place at the neckline and armhole edges to the main fabric bodice.

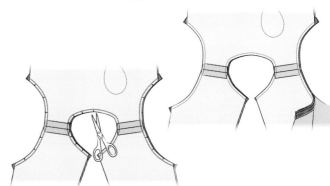

4. Lay the lining-fabric bodice out flat on your work surface, right side up, and place the main fabric on top, right side down. Pin around the neckline and armholes. Resew over the original stitch lines.

5. Snip into the curved seam allowances, press the seams open, and turn the bodice through.

6. Pin the side seams, with the right sides of the dress and right side of the lining together, carefully matching the armhole seams. Sew in a continuous seam on each side, taking care that the piping joins exactly and is facing in the same direction against the seam for each side of the dress. Press.

BALLOON APPLIQUÉ

1. On the right side of the skirt front, mark the positions of the balloons, then, using tailor's chalk, draw freehand lines across the skirt to mark the positions of the balloons' strings.

2. Sew lengths of the narrow tape or ribbon along the marked lines.

3. Bond adhesive web to the wrong sides of the contrast fabrics for the balloons (see page 13). Using the template on page 209, cut out one balloon from each colour.

4. Peel off the backing paper and apply the balloons to the skirt. Cover with a cloth and heat-press (see page 13). Stitch around the balloons close to the edges.

5. If desired, use the coloured ribbons to make little bows for the balloons' ties, and sew them in place.

BUNTING HEM DECORATION (OPTIONAL)

1. Cut 16 rectangles of contrast fabric in different colours, each 12 × 7cm (4¾ × 2¾in).

2. Fold each rectangle in half crossways then fold the left and right corner inwards to the centre to create little triangles.

3. Press.

4. Arrange the pieces along the hem of the skirt, equally spacing the colours and with right sides of the skirt fabric facing the side of each triangle with the folded centre. Pin and then sew in place. Overlock the hem edge.

SKIRT

1. Overlock the side edges and lower edge of the main-fabric skirt and lining-fabric skirt.

2. Gather the top edge of the main-fabric skirt (see page 18) until it is the same length as the lower edge of the bodice. Take your time so that you don't snap any of the threads. Repeat for the lining-fabric skirt.

(CON'T)

JOINING

1. Pin the gathered edge of the main-fabric skirt to the lower edge of the main-fabric bodice, right sides together and raw edges even, starting and finishing at centre back; stitch. Repeat for the lining-fabric skirt and bodice. Overlock the seams if desired.

2. Mark the length of your zip along the opening from the top of the neckline downwards into the skirt.

3. Pin the centre back edges of the main-fabric skirt with right sides together, and sew from the bottom edge up to this marked point. Repeat for the lining-fabric skirt. Press the seams open and continue to press the seam allowances open all the way to the top of the zip opening.

INSERTING THE ZIP

1. Insert an invisible zip (see page 19) or plain zip (see page 24) into the main-fabric dress.

2. Hand stitch the lining into place around the zip (or, if you prefer, carefully machine stitch it in place over the original stitching, through all the layers).

FINISHING

1. Hem the main-fabric skirt, with the bunting pointing downwards, and the seam pushed upwards into the skirt. Hem the lining.

2. Working from the inside of the dress, sew the main fabric to the lining at regular intervals along the waistline to prevent movement. You may prefer to sew this by hand.

3. For the sash, fold the cotrast fabric in half lengthways, right sides together. Pin and stitch across the ends and along the long edge, leaving an opening of 10cm (4in). Press the seams open, snip off the corners of the seam allowances, and turn through. Press, and hand sew the opening closed.

MAKING A GATHERED SKIRT

To adapt this project to make a gathered skirt, follow the instructions for Cutting out, Balloon Appliqué, and Skirt, and use the sash pattern to create a tied waistband. (If you want to tie the skirt at the sides, you will need to adjust the positions of the balloons.)

1. Prepare the waistband by pressing under 1 cm (³⁄₈in) on all edges, then folding it in half lengthways, wrong sides together, and pressing.

2. On the waistband, mark a length equal to your child's waist measurement, leaving an equal amount at each end.

3. Gather the waist line to the required size (see page 18). Repeat for the lining (if required).

4. Pin and stitch the side seam of the main-fabric skirt, leaving 5cm (2in) unstitched at the top, to allow the skirt to be taken off and put on easily without the need for a zip. Press the seam allowances back on the unstitched portion. Repeat for the lining skirt.

5. Sew outer and inner skirts together at the waistline, with all seams concealed, ready to add the waistband.

6. Unfold one turned-in edge of the waistband and pin the right side of the waistband to the wrong side of the gathered main-fabric skirt, with raw edges even and the marked lines on the band even with the side edges of the skirt. Stitch along the fold line of the waistband. Press the seam allowance and gathers towards the waistband.

7. Fold the waistband over to the front of the skirt, with the pressed-under edge turned under. Pin and topstitch the waistband in place, covering the previous stitching. Continue stitching along the waistband beyond the edges of the skirt, and across the ends, forming the ties.

8. Hem the lower edge of both the main-fabric skirt and the lining skirt.

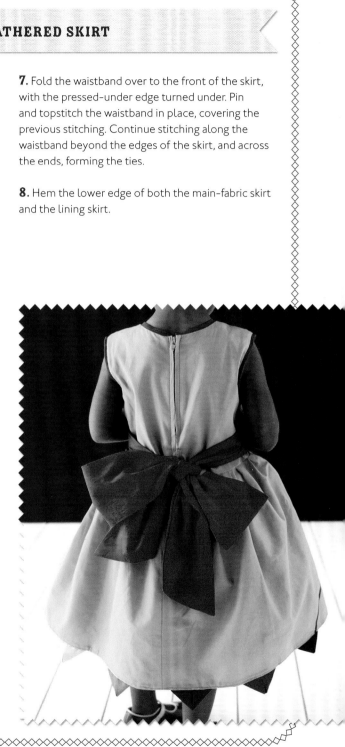

RAINBOW TWIRLING DRESS

Fun and frivolous, this stunning dress is ideal for summer festivals. It is best made from jersey but woven fabric will also work. Choose rainbow shades for the circle skirt, which is perfect for twirling and looks great worn with bright leggings. The elasticated waist makes it easy to get on and off, without the need for a zip.

YOU WILL NEED

Party dress bodice and skater skirt patterns

Jersey fabric in rainbow colours – enough to make 8 skirt panels, each 45cm × 45cm (17½ x 17½ in)

Contrast jersey for the welts

Jersey fabric for the front and back bodice

Matching fabric for the waistband

5mm – (¼in –) wide elastic

Matching sewing thread

Tailor's chalk

CUTTING OUT

> **TIP**
> If sourcing coloured jersey proves difficult, you could use simple plain T-shirts instead.

This unlined dress is finished at the neckline and armholes with welts.

NOTE: Seam allowances are 1cm (³⁄8in) unless otherwise specified.

1. Choose the best size for your child, using the guide on page 26. Trace the pattern for the party dress bodice available online (see page 11) following the lines for the correct size. Trace the pattern for the skater skirt also available online, following the lines for the correct size. Make patterns for the bodice front, bodice back (but without a centre back seam) and skirt panels.

2. Press the fabric pieces for the skirt and lay them on a flat surface. Position the pattern on the fabric, selecting the correct number to achieve a multi-coloured effect. Mark around the pattern using tailor's chalk, adding 1cm (³⁄8in) all around for seam allowances. Repeat for the bodice front and back.

3. For the welts, cut three 6.5cm – (2½in –) wide strips of contrast jersey fabric across the width of the fabric.

(CON'T)

JOINING

1. Lay out, pin and stitch all the skirt panels together along the side edges, right sides together, in the desired sequence. Use a stretch stitch or a setting on your machine that will stitch the seams and finish the edges, referring to page 23 and your machine manual. Overlock all the edges if desired.

4. Pin the welts to the neck opening and armholes, right sides together, matching the underarm seams and easing the loops to provide a small amount of stretch. Stitch using the same stretch stitch as in step 1.

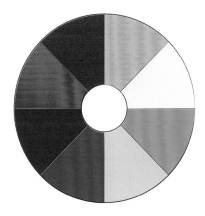

2. Using the same stretch stitch, pin, sew and overlock the shoulder seams and side seams of the bodice, right sides together.

3. Lay the bodice flat and measure the armhole and neck opening. Reduce these measurements by 10 per cent, and cut the three fabric strips to these lengths. Pin and stitch the ends, right sides together, forming loops. I've seamed a second colour within the neck welt for detail.

5. Pin the lower edge of the bodice to the top edge of the skirt, right sides together, easing into place if necessary. Using the same stretch stitch, sew and overlock together.

6. Stitch the elastic to the seam, gently pulling the elastic to create a soft gather (see page 18).

TIP
Take care that each skirt panel uses the same grain line, so that the bias of the fabric will not warp the seams.

MERMAID STORYTIME SUNDRESS

Little ones are introduced to the mythical imagery of mermaids through classic tales from an early age. What little girl wouldn't want to dress like a mermaid? This simple crossover-back sundress is a true labour of love. Making the individual scales takes time but is worth the effort. I've added some gold scales as well, to add shimmer. The crossover back makes the design easy to fit, and the shape could be used to create a simple alternative sundress without the scales. It is sure to turn heads on holiday.

YOU WILL NEED

Mermaid dress pattern

Scale and scallop shell templates

70cm (27½in) fabric for the dress and straps

70cm (27½in) lining fabric

Contrast fabric in shades of blue and green for scales

Gold or silver fabric for the scallop shell appliqué

30cm (12in) square of iron-on double-sided adhesive web

Matching sewing thread

Tailor's chalk

CUTTING OUT

This lined sundress has straps secured through buttonholes at the back.

NOTE: Seam allowances are 1cm (3/8in) unless otherwise specified.

1. Choose the best size for your child, using the guide on page 26. Trace the pattern for the mermaid dress available online (see page 11), following the lines for the correct size. Make patterns for the bodice front, bodice back and three skirt panels.

2. Press the fabric and arrange it on a flat surface, so you can cut out one bodice front, one bodice back and one each of the three skirt panels. Mark or number the skirt panels in order.

3. Mark around the pattern pieces using tailor's chalk, adding 1cm (3/8in) all around for seam allowances, and 2cm (3/4in) at the hem. Cut out the pieces carefully.

4. Because the dress is lined, you will need to cut a complete new dress from lining fabric, but you can cut the three skirt panels as one large piece – just don't forget to omit the seam allowances between the panels. The lining dress should be at least 2cm (3/4in) shorter.

(CON'T)

SCALES & SCALLOP SHELLS

1. Using the scale template on the pattern, cut out about 80 scales from the contrast fabrics. Pin two semicircles with right sides together, and sew around the curved edge, 1cm (³/₈in) from the edge. Snip into the seam allowances as shown, and turn through. Press. Repeat to make about 40 scales in total.

2. Bond adhesive web (see page 13) to the wrong side of the scallop shell fabric. Using the scallop shell template on page 209, cut out two scallop shells. Peel off the paper backing, position the shells on the bodice front, and heat-press in place (see page 13). Stitch close to the edges of the shells and also along the lines indicated on the template.

TIP
Another way to make scales would be to cut semicircles from felt and sew the single-layer felt scales to the skirt. Increase the dramatic effect by being more generous with the number of scales.

STRAPS

1. For the straps, cut out two fabric strips using the pattern available online (see page 11).

2. Press under 1cm (³/₈in) on each edge. Fold in half lengthways, wrong sides together, and topstitch down both long edges and across one end.

JOINING

1. Pin the bodice front to the bodice back at one side edge, right sides together. Sew and then press the seam open.

2. Repeat step 1 for each of the three skirt panels, and arrange on a flat surface.

3. Pin the scales in position on the right side of the skirt panels, with raw edges even, and placing them no closer than 1cm (3/8in) from the side edges of the panels. Stitch in place close to the straight edge of each scale.

4. Pin the long edges of the skirt panels with right sides together in the right sequence. Stitch the seams.

5. Pin the top edge of the skirt to the lower edge of the bodice, matching the unstitched side edges. Stitch and overlock the seam.

6. Right sides together, pin the unstitched side edge of the bodice front to that of the bodice back, and the side edge of the skirt front and back, matching the horizontal seams. Stitch as one continuous seam. Overlock the edges.

7. Overlock the lower edge of the skirt, and press under 1cm (3/8in). Stitch.

LINING

1. Sew the side seams of the lining, and the lining skirt; overlock. Hem the lower edge.

2. Place the finished dress inside the lining, right sides together. Pin along the top edge. Sandwich the open end of each strap between the main fabric and lining, at the positions marked on the pattern, with the raw edge of the strap even with the top edge of the bodice. Stitch along the top edge. Turn back and press, then topstitch all around.

FINISHING

1. At each side of the centre back, sew a buttonhole large enough to thread the strap through (see page 15).

2. Thread the two straps through the opposite buttonhole so that the straps cross over at the back, and tie at centre back.

BUTTERFLY SUNDRESS & BONNET

With its dainty, traditional look, this sundress has an heirloom feel. Made in white linen, it is perfect for summer parties or special occasions but would look equally good in bright shades. The butterfly bonnet makes a whimsical addition for a baby and can double as a sun hat.

SUNDRESS

YOU WILL NEED

Butterfly dress pattern

70cm (27½in) fabric

Contrast fabric in varying colours for wing details

30cm (12in) square of iron-on double-sided adhesive web

2 buttons, 2cm (¾in) in diameter

Rickrack trim (optional)

Matching sewing thread

Tailor's chalk

CUTTING OUT

This unlined sundress has shoulder straps with attached 'butterfly wings' and a double-button fastening at the back.

NOTE: Seam allowances are 1cm (³/₈in) unless otherwise specified.

1. Choose the best size for your child, using the guide on page 26. Trace the pattern for the butterfly dress available online (see page 11), following the lines for the correct size. Make a pattern for the bodice front, bodice back, skirt panel and strap.

2. Press the fabric and arrange it on a flat surface so you can cut out two bodice fronts, two bodice backs, two skirt panels and four straps. Make sure the centre front and centre back are parallel to the selvedge.

3. Mark around the pattern pieces using tailor's chalk, adding 1cm (³/₈in) all around for seam allowances, and 2cm (¾in) at the hem. Cut out the pieces carefully.

(CON'T)

WINGS

1. Using the pattern available online (see page 11), cut out two pairs of shoulder wings from the dress fabric.

2. Bond adhesive web to the wrong side of the wing-detail fabric scraps (see page 13) and follow the pattern to cut out four pairs of details from these scraps. Peel off the backing paper from two pairs of details, and position one pair of details on one shoulder wing from each pair of wings. Heat-press them in place (see page 13). Stitch around the edges.

3. For each shoulder wing, pin a decorated piece to a plain piece, right sides together, around the scalloped edge; stitch.

4. Snip into the seam allowances as shown, and turn through. Press.

5. For the back wings, bond adhesive web to the wrong side of a piece of dress fabric large enough for the back wings. Peel off the backing paper and bond the wrong side of a second dress-fabric piece to it. This creates a stable fabric from which you can cut the wings without the need for fiddly sewing. Using the pattern, cut out the back wings.

6. Peel off the backing paper from the remaining two pairs of wing details from step 2, and position them on the back wings. Heat-press in place, then stitch around all edges of the details.

PIN TUCKS & STRAPS

1. Mark on the bodice front the positions of the pin tucks shown on the pattern. Fold the bodice front vertically along each pin tuck line in turn and sew 2mm from the edge. Press so that they are facing outwards from the centre front and are spaced evenly. Check the pinned neckline against the pattern for the facing to make sure the size is right. Stitch in place a fraction less than 1cm (³/₈in) from the edge.

2. Now assemble the wing straps. On the outer edge of the two strap pieces, mark the position of the shoulder wings shown on the strap pattern. Pin each shoulder wing to the corresponding strap, right sides together. Now take the second strap piece for each wing strap, and, placing right sides facing together, sew along the same line to sandwich the wing within the strap layers. Stitch then press the seam open.

3. Press under 1cm (³/₈in) on the opposite long edge and on the end that will be at the back.

4. For each wing strap, topstitch the layers together down the longer end and at one short end, as indicated on the pattern.

JOINING

1. Overlock the edges of the skirt front and back.

2. Pin the two skirt panels with right sides together at one side edge only; stitch, then press the seam open.

3. Gather the top edge of the skirt to the required length (see page 18), as indicated on the pattern.

4. Pin one bodice front to one bodice back on the same side as for the skirt in step 2; stitch, then press the seam open. Repeat for the other bodice front and bodice back, to form a facing.

5. Pin the (unstitched) strap front ends to the top edge of the bodice front, right sides together and raw edges even as marked on the pattern. Place the bodice facing to the edge of the main bodice, with the straps sandwiched between the bodice front and the facing. Pin and stitch along the front and back top edges. Press the seams open, then flatten.

6. Pin the bodice to the skirt, right sides together. Seam these together with the gathered skirt edges uppermost as you sew. Press the raw gathered edges upward into the bodice.

7. Overlock the lower edge of the facing.

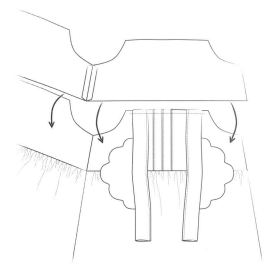

8. Now sew the entire open side seam continuously through the skirt, bodice and facing. Press open the seams and press the bodice again.

9. To secure the facing, pin the bodice facing to the bodice, wrong sides together, trapping the raw edges inside. Sew close to the bodice edge with the right side of the dress uppermost.

10. Carefully topstitch 5mm (¼in) from the neck, armhole and lower edges of the bodice.

FINISHING

1. Hem the dress, and add a row of rickrack trim if desired.

2. Mark two equally spaced buttonholes in the centre of each back strap end. Make the buttonholes (see page 15) to a suitable size.

3. Sew two buttons on the inside of the bodice back, so that the straps can be either crossed at the back or worn straight down. The two buttonholes on each strap will ensure that the dress fits either way.

4. Attach the back wing piece to the centre back of the bodice, either sewing it in place or using a large safety pin so that the wings can be removed when the dress is washed.

BUTTERFLY BONNET

YOU WILL NEED

Butterfly bonnet pattern

30cm (12in) fabric30cm (12in) lining fabric (or use self-fabric)

Contrast fabric in varying colours for butterfly detail

30cm (12in) square of iron-on double-sided adhesive web

90cm (35½in) ribbon for ties (or use self-fabric)

Matching sewing thread

Tailor's chalk

CUTTING OUT

This lined bonnet consists of three panels, tied at the chin.

NOTE: Seam allowances are 1cm (³⁄₈in) unless otherwise specified.

1. Choose the best size for your child, using the guide below. Trace the pattern for the butterfly bonnet available online (see page 11), following the lines for the correct size. Make a pattern for the side panel and central gusset.

2. Press the fabric and arrange it on a flat surface so you can cut out two side panels and one central gusset from the main fabric for the outer bonnet, and the same from the lining fabric (or self-fabric) for the inner bonnet. Make sure the grain lines and centre front line are parallel to the selvedge.

3. Mark around the pattern pieces using tailor's chalk, adding 1cm (³⁄₈in) all around for seam allowances. Cut out the pieces carefully.

SIZE GUIDE	
Size	**Age**
XS	6 months
S	1–3 years
M	3–5 years
L	5–7 years

WINGS & TIES

1. Using the pattern, make two wings in the same way as for the shoulder wings of the Sundress, steps 1–4.

2. If using self-fabric for the ties, cut two 30 × 4cm (12 × 1½in) strips of fabric on the bias. Press under 1cm (⅜in) on both long edges and one end of each tie, then fold in half lengthways and stitch close to the edges.

ASSEMBLING

1. Pin the two side panels of the hat on either side of the centre gusset, with right sides together. Stitch both seams and press open. Repeat for the lining.

2. Pin the outer hat to the lining, right sides together and matching the seam lines. Pin a tie in place on each side at the positions marked, sandwiched between the outer hat and the lining, with raw edges even. Stitch all the way around the bonnet, leaving 8cm (3¼in) open at centre back. Snip into the curved seam allowances and turn through.

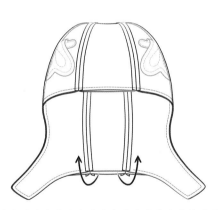

FINISHING

1. Press the bonnet, rolling the fabric gently on the curved edges to obtain a good finish.

2. Topstitch 5mm (¼in) from the edge all the way around, stitching the opening at the back closed at the same time.

3. Sew the two wings into position on each of the bonnet sides, around the edges as marked on the pattern.

FLOWER PETAL ROMPER & SUN HAT

Cool and easy to wear during the summer, this charming little set can be made in heavier fabrics and layered with a long-sleeved top in cooler weather. This is a favourite of mine and has a nostalgic feel. Use a tiny print for the main fabric, such as this Liberty print, with contrast plain fabrics for the flowers, stem and leaves.

ROMPER

YOU WILL NEED

Romper and pocket patterns

Raindrop template

70cm (27½in) medium-weight print fabric

Contrast plain fabrics for flowers, stems and leaves

30cm (12in) square of iron-on double-sided adhesive web

1m (39in) narrow elastic

Matching sewing thread

Tailor's chalk

CUTTING OUT

SIZE GUIDE	
Size	**Age**
XS	6 months
S	1–3 years
M	3–5 years
L	5–7 years

NOTE: Seam allowances are 1cm (³⁄₈in) unless otherwise specified.

1. Choose the best size for your child, using the guide on page 26. Trace the pattern for the romper and pocket available online (see page 11), following the lines for the correct size. Make a pattern for half the front/back and the rounded pocket.

2. Press the print fabric and arrange it on a flat surface so you can cut out a right front/back and a left front/back. Make sure the grain lines are parallel to the selvedge and any pattern runs in the right direction.

(CON'T)

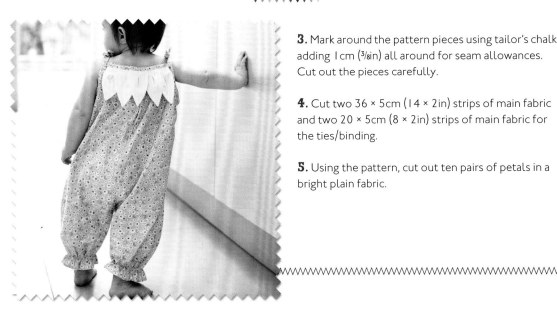

3. Mark around the pattern pieces using tailor's chalk, adding 1cm (³⁄₈in) all around for seam allowances. Cut out the pieces carefully.

4. Cut two 36 × 5cm (14 × 2in) strips of main fabric and two 20 × 5cm (8 × 2in) strips of main fabric for the ties/binding.

5. Using the pattern, cut out ten pairs of petals in a bright plain fabric.

PREPARING TIES & PETALS

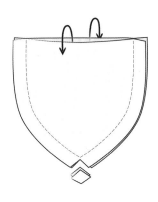

1. For the ties, press under 1cm (³⁄₈in) on the long edges of each of the four strips. Fold in half lengthways and press again, but do not stitch yet.

2. For the petals, pin the pairs with right sides together, and stitch 5mm (¹⁄₄in) from the curved edges. Snip into the curved seam allowances, turn through and press. At the top edge of each, fold in half lengthwise, right sides together, and stitch 5mm (¹⁄₄in) from the fold for 2cm (³⁄₄in), creating a tuck.

ASSEMBLY & APPLIQUÉ

1. Right sides together, pin the left front/back to the right front/back at centre front. Stitch the seam, overlock and press.

2. Bond adhesive web to the wrong side of the contrast fabric for the stem and leaves (see page 13). Cut out several 5–7mm (about ¹⁄₄in) strips for the stem. Using the raindrop template on page 215, cut out two leaves.

3. Using tailor's chalk, carefully draw a curved line from the neck to the left leg hem of the romper front, using the photo on page 72 as a guide. Peel off the backing paper from the fabric strips and heat-press along the line, gently easing them into the curve as you go, and making the ends meet to create a continuous line. Topstitch in place.

POCKETS

1. Using the pattern provided, cut a pocket from matching or contrast fabric, and overlock the edges. Fold and press the curved edge under by 5mm (¼in). Now fold and press under the top edge on each pocket by 1cm (⅜in); topstitch. Thread a length of narrow elastic equal to the width of the pocket through this channel in the pocket top to secure at one end. Gently gather and stitch at the opposite end to create a gathered top. Trim away the excess elastic.

2. Pin the pocket in position on the romper front at one side, as shown in the photo. Topstitch around the side and bottom edges, reinforcing the start and finish with a small triangle.

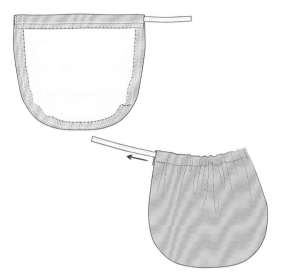

LEGS

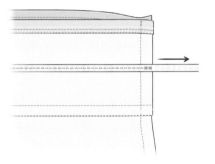

1. Overlock the remaining leg edges. Turn under 5mm (¼in) at the lower edge of each leg and stitch. Mark a line above each leg hem, as indicated on the pattern and sew a 22cm (9in) length of narrow elastic to the line, stretching it gently as you go (see page 18). You may need a little more or less elastic, depending on leg size.

2. Pin the inside leg seam, right sides together. Stich the seam, overlock and press.

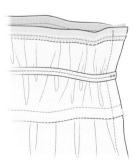

JOINING

1. Sew the centre back seam and overlock.

2. Place the legs right sides together and sew from one ankle to the other, finishing at the start and end with a backstitch.

FINISHING

1. Gather the back neck edge and front neck edge to measure 19cm (7½in) (see page 18).

2. Pin the petals in place along the back and front neck edge on the right side, overlapping the petals slightly.

3. Open out one fold on the shorter binding strips, and use to bind the front and back neck edges (see page 14).

4. Mark the centre of each longer tie, and position each mark at an underarm seam. Open out one fold on the longer binding strips, and use to bind the underarm edges (see page 14), but this time stitch along the entire length of the ties.

SUN HAT

YOU WILL NEED

Flower petal sun hat pattern

25cm (10in) medium-weight print fabric

Contrast plain fabrics for petals

Contrast fabric for lining (or use self-fabric)

Scrap of contrast fabric or ribbon for loop at top

Matching sewing thread

Tailor's chalk

SIZE GUIDE	
Size	**Age**
XS	6 months
S	1–3 years
M	3–5 years
L	5–7 years

CUTTING OUT

This sun hat consists of six panels, with flower petals forming a brim.

1. Choose the best size for your child, using the guide on page 76. Trace the pattern for the flower petal sun hat online (see page 11), following the lines for the correct size. Accuracy is really important, as the six panels are small, and a variation in the seam allowance will alter the size of the hat. Make a pattern for the panel.

2. Press the print fabric and arrange it on a flat surface so you can cut out six panels for the outer hat, and the same from the lining fabric (or self-fabric) for the inner hat. Make sure the grain lines are parallel to the selvedge and any pattern runs in the right direction.

3. Mark around the pattern pieces using tailor's chalk, adding 1 cm (³⁄₈in) all around for seam allowances. Cut out the pieces carefully.

4. Using the pattern, cut out eight pairs of petals from a bright contrast fabric.

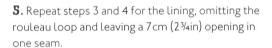

MAKING THE HAT

1. Prepare the petals as for the romper (see Preparing Ties & Petals, step 2, page 74).

2. Make a rouleau loop (see page 22) from a scrap of contrast fabric or a piece of fine ribbon.

3. Pin the three panels from one half of the hat together in the correct order, right sides together, and stitch the seams. Repeat for the other three panels.

5. Repeat steps 3 and 4 for the lining, omitting the rouleau loop and leaving a 7 cm (2³⁄₄in) opening in one seam.

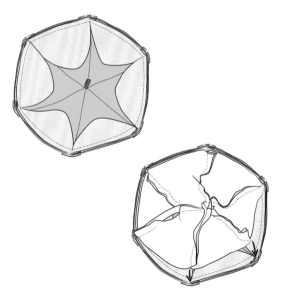

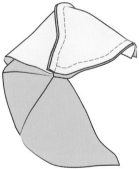

4. Pin one half of the hat to the other half, right sides together. Insert the rouleau loop between them, halfway along the seam, with raw edges even. Stitch the seam.

6. Pin the petals to the edge of the outer hat, right sides together and raw edges even. Stitch all around.

7. Pull the hat through the opening in the lining. Press, then sew the opening closed.

LADYBIRD BABY BUBBLE ROMPER

This adorable little ladybird baby romper is perfect for lazy summer days. Similar to the bumblee shortie romper in my first book, *Wild Things*, the romper is layered to give the effect of wings. To make it into a dress, simply alter the under-section by cutting straight down to the hemline and eliminating the knicker shaping. You might also like to adapt the wings and make the design into a butterfly.

YOU WILL NEED

Romper and ladybird wings patterns

70cm (27½yd) medium-weight red/white spot fabric

25cm (10in) contrast black cotton for yoke and spots

Red fabric for wings

Iron-on double-sided adhesive web

Interfacing (optional)

1m (39in) 1cm- (³⁄₈in–) wide elastic

Soft wadding or toy filling for antennae (or use soft fabric scraps)

2 contrast buttons, about 2cm (³⁄₄in) in diameter, for eyes

Matching sewing thread

Tailor's chalk

CUTTING OUT

NOTE: Seam allowances are 1cm (³⁄₈in) unless otherwise specified.

1. Choose the best size for your child, using the guide on page 26. Trace the pattern for the romper available online (see page 11), following the lines for the correct size. Make a pattern for half the front/back. Make a pattern for the ladybird wings.

SIZE GUIDE	
Size	**Age**
XS	6 months
S	1–3 years
M	3–5 years

(CON'T)

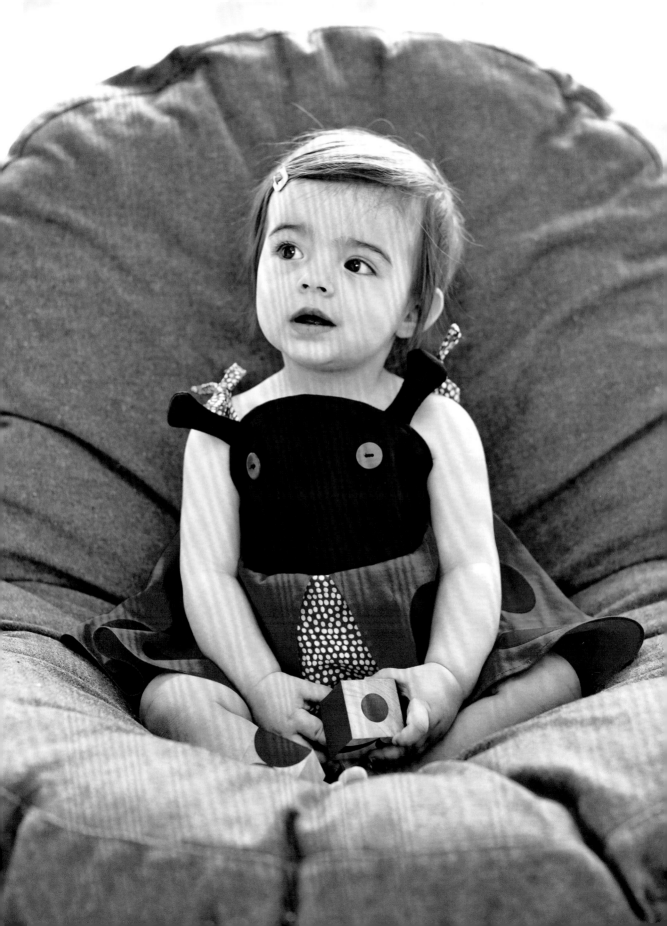

2. Press the red/white spot or your chosen main fabric and arrange it on a flat surface so you can cut out a right front/back and a left front/back. Make sure the grain lines are parallel to the selvedge and any pattern runs in the right direction.

3. Mark around the romper pattern piece using tailor's chalk, adding 1cm (³⁄₈in) all around for seam allowances. Cut out the pieces carefully.

4. Trace the pattern for the romper face and the antennae, following the lines for the correct size.

Make a pattern for the face and the antennae. From the black fabric, cut two face panels and four antenna pieces, adding 1cm (³⁄₈in) all around for seam allowances.

5. From the plain red fabric, cut two wings.

6. From the red/white spot fabric, cut out two 30 × 5cm (12 × 2in) strips for the front ties, two 35 × 5cm (14 × 2in) strips and one 20cm (8in) strip to bind the back yoke.

ANTENNAE & SPOTS

1. Place two antenna pieces right sides together, and sew around the keyhole-shaped edge, leaving the other end open. Snip into the curved seam allowances and turn through. Using a pencil, gently fill the antenna with soft wadding or toy filling. Repeat for the second antenna.

2. To prepare the spots, bond adhesive web to the wrong side of the black cotton (see page 13). Cut circles from this and arrange them randomly over the wings. Peel off the backing paper and heat-press in place. Stitch down by stitching around the edge or in a cross shape through the centre of each circle.

3. Overlock the lower edge of each wing, and turn under a narrow hem. Stitch.

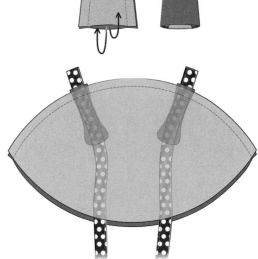

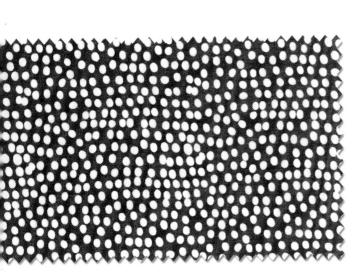

TIES & YOKE FACE

1. For the front ties, press under 5mm (¼in) on each long edge and one end of the two shorter strips. Fold them in half lengthways, wrong sides together, and press again. Stitch around the folded edges. Repeat for the two back ties.

2. Place the two yoke face panels with right sides together. If desired, back one of them with interfacing or an additional layer of fabric to make the yoke more substantial. Insert the open ends of the two front ties and the two antennae between the layers, raw edges even. Pin around the top edge of the yoke, and stitch.

3. Snip into the curved seam allowances, turn through and press.

ELASTICATING THE LEGS & ASSEMBLING

1. Place the main romper front and back pieces right sides facing and sew the side seams.

2. Overlock these seams, and the entire leg opening on both sides.

3. Sew the gusset seam together.

4. Prepare two cut lengths of narrow elastic according to the size you have used as indicated on the pattern. Join these at one end by sewing together carefully, so that you have an elastic loop.

5. To add this to the knicker leg edge, turn back each leg edge by 1 cm (³⁄₈in), trapping the elastic inside the channel. Sew all the way around as shown in the illustration. Take care not to sew into the elastic itself so that it finally runs freely within the channel you have created.

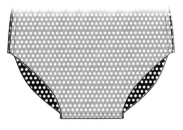

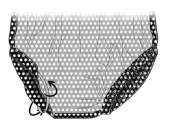

YOKE WINGS & BACK TIE

1. Place the wings into position onto the romper. Sew into place to secure.

2. Gather the top edge of the romper back to measure approximately 19cm (7½in) (see page 18).

3. Bind the gathered edge (see page 14).

4. Now finish the underarm/back strap. Take each longer strip and add to the underarm as a binding. Continue to sew to the end of the strap to finish, folding the raw edges inward at the end of the strap.

5. Pin the lower edge of the front yoke to the gathered top edge of the romper front, right sides together. Stitch in place. Press the seam towards the yoke. Overlock the lower edge of the yoke.

FINISHING

1. Press the yoke, then topstitch 5mm (¼in) from the edges.

2. Sew the button eyes in position on the yoke.

LITTLE CHICK REVERSIBLE APRON

I love the simplicity of this shape. It is a truly functional pinafore in every sense. It's reversible, making it ideal for messy play, and the deep pocket is perfect for gathering treasures. It adds a layer of warmth over everyday clothes and simple base layers such as leggings and tops, yet in the summer months it also looks lovely on its own, with just a pair of baby knickers or bloomers.

YOU WILL NEED

Reversible pinafore and pocket patterns

1 length each of 2 contrasting dress fabrics (see Calculating fabric lengths, below)

Contrast fabric for pockets

Assorted fabrics for chick details

30cm (12in) square of iron-on double-sided adhesive web

1 contrast button for chick's eye

Contrast rickrack trim for pocket edge

Matching and contrast sewing thread

Tailor's chalk

CUTTING OUT

This reversible pinafore has a crossover back.

NOTE: Seam allowances are 1cm (³⁄₈in) unless otherwise specified.

1. Choose the best size for your child, using the guide on page 26. Trace the pattern for the reversible pinafore available online (see page 11), following the lines for the correct size. Make a pattern for the front and another for the backs.

(CON'T)

CALCULATING FABRIC LENGTHS	6 MONTHS-3 YEARS	3-5 YEARS
Width 110cm (44in) dress	70cm (27½in)	80cm (31½in)
Width 150cm (60in) dress	70cm (27½in)	80cm (31½in)

2. Press the first fabric and arrange it on a flat surface so you can cut out a whole front and two back pieces. Make sure the centre front and the grain lines of the backs are parallel to the selvedge.

3. Mark around the pattern pieces using tailor's chalk, adding 1cm (³⁄₈in) all around for seam allowances, and 2cm (³⁄₄in) at the hem. Cut out the pieces carefully.

4. Repeat steps 1–3 for the second fabric.

5. Using the pocket pattern available online (see page 11), make a pattern for the plain pocket. On the contrast fabric, mark around the pattern piece using tailor's chalk, adding 1cm (³⁄₈in) all around for seam allowances. Cut out two single pockets.

POCKETS & APPLIQUÉ

1. Overlock the edges of all pockets if desired. Press under 1cm (³⁄₈in) on the side and lower edges. Stitch rickrack trim around the curved edge.

2. Mark the chick pocket's position on the right side of one pinafore front with tailor's chalk. For the chick-pocket decorations, bond adhesive web to the wrong side of the scraps (see page 13), then turn them over and, using the templates on page 209, draw the feathers, wing, coxcomb and beak on the fabric side. Cut out. Peel off the backing paper and arrange the feathers, coxcomb and beak in the correct positions on the pinafore front, adhesive side down. Heat-press to bond.

3. Create legs from folded strips of fabric, and sew in place on the pinafore front.

4. Sew the wing in place on the chick pocket. Pin the chick pocket to the dress front. Topstitch around the side and bottom edges, backstitching at the start and finish.

5. On the two plain pockets, press under 1cm (³⁄₈in) twice on the top edge; topstitch.

6. Mark the plain pockets' position on the right side of the other pinafore front with tailor's chalk. Pin and topstitch the plain pockets in place around the side and bottom edges, backstitching at the start and finish to secure.

JOINING

1. Pin the pinafore backs to the front along the side edges, right sides together, and stitch. Press the seam open. Topstitch the side seams if required, especially if you are using denim, to create a utility feel.

2. On a flat surface, place one pinafore on top of the other, right sides together. Pin all the way around the edge, tacking if desired. Mark the positions for the straps, as shown on the patterns. Stitch around the edges, leaving openings for the straps where marked, leaving the hem entirely open. (Sewing around the curved edges can be tricky, so take your time, gently rotating the fabric a little as you go, with the needle in the fabric and the machine foot raised, then lower the foot again before stitching.)

4. Lay the pinafore out flat, with the back crossing. Placing your hand inside the pinafore and up through one of the strap openings, grab hold of the strap and pull it through while keeping a firm hold on it. Repeat for the other straps. Pin then sew each strap in place.

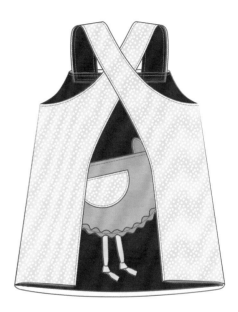

5. Now continue to sew the hem with right sides together, leaving a 20cm (8in) opening. Pull the apron through to the right sides and press.

3. Carefully snip the curved seam allowances, to within 2mm of the seam. This helps to give a good curved finish. Snip excess fabric from the corners of the strap seam allowances. Turn through carefully and press.

FINISHING

1. Topstitch around the arm and neck edges, 5mm (¼in) from the edges, using a contrast thread and closing the opening at the hem as you go. Take extra care when stitching around the curves. Lay the pinafore flat, and press.

2. Sew a button to the chick pocket to form an eye.

LITTLE GODDESS DRESS

Perfect for role play, this apron dress has a touch of nostalgia and is so cute worn on its own in the summer, with little sun-kissed shoulders.

YOU WILL NEED

Waistband, skirt, bib and strap patterns

1 length of dress fabric, 110cm (44in) or 150cm (60in) wide for outer skirt (see Calculating fabric lengths, below)

Plain fabric for pockets, approximately 1 fat quarter

Iron-on double-sided adhesive web or iron-on interfacing (optional)

30cm (12in) elastic 2.5cm (1in) wide

2 buttons

Jumbo rickrack for the bib trim

Matching sewing thread

Tailor's chalk

CUTTING OUT

NOTE: Seam allowances are 1cm (³/₈in) unless otherwise specified.

1. Measure your child's waist and make a pattern for the waistband. Cut two waistband fronts and two backs.

2. If your fabric is lightweight, you may wish to strengthen the waistband with an 8cm- (3¼in-) wide strip of iron-on adhesive web or interfacing, cut to the same length as the waistband.

3. Create a pattern for the skirt, according to your child's size, and cut a skirt front and back.

4. Trace the patterns for the bib and straps available online (see page 11). Make a pattern for the bib. Mark around the pattern using tailor's chalk, adding 1cm (³/₈in) all around for the seam allowance. Cut out a bib front and a bib back, making sure the grain lines are parallel to the selvedge. Also cut out two straps.

5. Using the heart pattern available online (see page 11), cut out four pocket pieces.

(CON'T)

CALCULATING FABRIC LENGTHS	6 MONTHS-3 YEARS	3-5 YEARS
Width 110cm (44in) dress	70cm (27½in)	80cm (31½in)
Width 150cm (60in) dress	70cm (27½in)	80cm (31½in)

POCKETS

1. Pin two pocket pieces with right sides together, and stitch all the way around, leaving a small opening at the lower edge through which to turn or bag the pocket through. Snip the centre of the heart at the seam, turn through and press.

2. Pin in position on the skirt, and topstitch along the sides, leaving the top open and backstitching at the start and finish.

3. Press under 1 cm (³/₈in) on both long edges and one end of each strap. Fold the straps in half lengthwise, wrong sides together, and topstitch close to the edges, leaving the unpressed end on each open.

4. Add the rickrack trim to the edges of the heart-shaped bib by trapping it between both layers. Trim the curves, including the point at the centre of the heart, then turn through and press. Sew away the excess rickrack at the centre front on the inside, as shown.

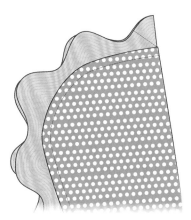

WAISTBAND & JOINING

1. Overlock both skirt pieces at the sides and hem. Assemble the front waistband by placing the bib between the inner and outer waistband as marked on the pattern.

2. Gather the top of the front of the skirt to size.

3. With the right side of the inner waistband facing the inside of the skirt, sew along the top to join the two layers. Now bring the waistband forward, press the remaining raw edge inward by 1 cm (³⁄₈in). Pin to the front face of the skirt and topstitch to assemble.

4. Assemble the back waistband by placing the premade straps between the inner and outer waistband, as marked on the pattern. Overlock the inner waistband raw edge.

5. Place the dress front and back together and sew the side seams. (At the waist sides, the inner back waistband will be loose.) Bring this around so that all of the raw edges are trapped inside, as shown.

6. Press the seams open.

7. Take the length of elastic and sew each end to one of the waist sides on the inside. Pin the waistband back into place.

8. Now with the right side of the skirt uppermost, gently stretch the waistband, and topstitch through to close the waistband along the entire back. There will be sufficient stretch for your child to easily pull the skirt on.

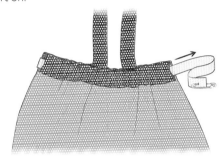

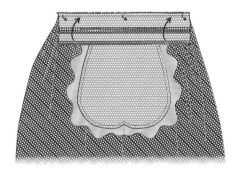

FINISHING

1. Press under a 2 cm (³⁄₄in) hem on both the outer skirt and the underskirt, and stitch. Stitch rickrack trim to the hem of the outer skirt if desired.

2. Try the dress on your child, crossing the straps at the back. Add a buttonhole to the end of each strap, and sew buttons to the inside of the waistband (see pages 15 and 16).

CHARACTER OUTFITS

BUNNY RABBIT CHARACTER DRESS

A classic character dress, made here in corduroy, this can also be the basis for other animals shown in this book. The large inner ears are a good opportunity to use precious or upcycled fabrics, which you can also add to the pocket tops. The large pompom tail is easy to make from yarn, and children enjoy helping. Making them reminds me of childhood.

YOU WILL NEED

Character dress patterns: front, back, yoke, straps and pockets

Rabbit face templates

1 length of soft, medium-weight woven cotton, such as corduroy, velvet or cotton twill (see Calculating fabric lengths, below)

Scraps of cotton in pale pink, floral print and dark grey

Scraps of white felt

Plain cotton or interfacing (optional)

30cm (12in) square of iron-on double-sided adhesive web

2 buttons

Matching sewing thread

Yarn for pompom

Cardboard for pompom

Tailor's chalk

CUTTING OUT

This unlined dress has a front yoke and shoulder straps, and is finished with front and back facings.

NOTE: Seam allowances are 1cm (³⁄₈in) unless otherwise specified.

1. Choose the best size for your child, using the guide on page 26. Trace the pattern for the character dress, front yoke, back facing, straps and pockets available online (see page 11), following the lines for the correct size and including the side extensions for the dress back.

(CON'T)

CALCULATING FABRIC LENGTHS	6 MONTHS–3 YEARS	3–5 YEARS
110cm (44in)	1m (39in)	120cm (47in)
150cm (60in)	80cm (31½in)	1m (39in)

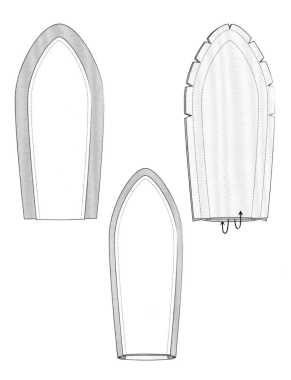

2. Press the main fabric and arrange it on a flat surface so you can cut out one dress front, one dress back, one back facing, two yokes and four straps. Make sure the grain lines on the pattern are parallel to the selvedge and that any pile is running in the right direction.

3. Mark around the pattern pieces using tailor's chalk, adding 1cm (³/₈in) all around for seam allowances, and 2cm (³/₄in) at the hem. Cut out the pieces carefully.

4. Cut out two pockets from the main fabric or a contrast fabric with a 1cm (³/₈in) seam allowance.

5. If the front yoke needs a little extra weight, cut another one from plain cotton or interfacing.

6. Using the rabbit face template on page 210, cut four ears from the main fabric, adding 1cm (³/₈in) all around for seam allowances. Cut two pocket trims, each 6cm (2¹/₄in) by the width of the pocket, from the floral print fabric.

YOKE

1. Bond adhesive web to the wrong side of the print fabric for the inner ears (see page 13). Using the inner ear template on page 210, cut out two inner ears.

2. Peel the backing paper off the adhesive web and position the inner ears on the right side of two ear pieces, as shown on the template, adhesive side down. Heat-press to fuse into place (see page 13). Using matching thread, topstitch the inner ear into place, 2mm from the edges.

3. Pin the two ear fronts to the two ear backs, right sides together, and sew 1cm (³/₈in) from the edges, leaving them open at the bottom edge. Trim a small triangle shape at the tip of the ear, close to the seam, to give a neat, pointed finish. Turn through and press from the reverse side. Sew a small tuck into the base of the ear to make the ear more rigid.

4. Bond adhesive web to the wrong sides of a dark grey scrap and a pale pink scrap. Using the templates on page 210, cut out two dark grey eyes, six dark grey whiskers and a pale pink nose.

5. Peeling off the backing paper, arrange the nose, eyes and whiskers on the right side of one yoke piece. Cover with a cloth and heat-press. Stitch around the edges of the eyes and nose to secure. If this gets difficult, you can simply sew straight lines horizontally, then vertically, to create a cross shape.

6. Pin this yoke piece to the other, right sides together. Add interfacing to the wrong side of the front yoke if you wish. Pin the ears in place between the layers, with the raw edges even and the ear front next to the front yoke piece. Sew around the top curved edge of the yoke, 1cm (³/₈in) from the edge, trapping the ears in place as you go. Carefully snip the curved seam allowances, then turn through and press.

POCKETS

1. Overlock the edges of the pocket trim and press under 1cm (³⁄₈in) on all four edges. On the pocket, overlock the edges and then press under 2cm (³⁄₄in) on the top edge; topstitch. Press under 1cm (³⁄₈in) on the remaining edges. Pin the pockets to the right side of the dress front in the positions shown on the pattern.

2. Cut triangles of white felt for the claws, each 4 × 2cm (1¹⁄₂ × ³⁄₄in). Insert three claws under the edge of each pocket.

3. Topstitch the pockets in place along the side and bottom edges, stitching 5mm (¹⁄₄in) from the edge, backstitching at the start and finish, and making sure the claws are caught in the stitching.

JOINING & STRAPS

1. Pin the dress front to the dress back at the side edges, right sides together. Sew the side seams, overlock the edges and press the seams towards the back.

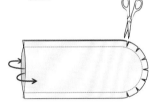

2. To make a strap, pin two strap pieces with right sides together and sew around the edges with a 1cm (³⁄₈in) seam allowance, leaving the straight, narrow end open. Snip into the curved seam allowances, then turn through and press. Topstitch around the edges. Repeat to make the other strap. Sew the two straps in place at the shoulders on the dress back, right sides together and raw edges even.

3. Sew the two tucks on the right side of the dress front, with the tucks open towards the outer edges.

4. Pin the lower edge of the prepared yoke to the top edge of the dress front, right sides together. Stitch. Overlock the edges, turn back and press.

5. Overlock the lower, curved edge of the back facing.

6. Pin the back facing to the dress back around outer edges, right sides together. Sew around outer edges, trapping the shoulder straps as you go. Carefully snip the curved seam allowances and trim the corners. Turn through and press. Slipstitch the shorter facing edges to the dress side seams.

(CON'T)

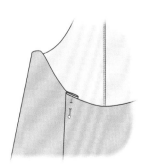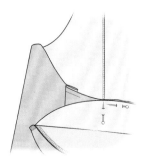

FINISHING

1. Topstitch 5mm (¼in) from the edge all the way around.

2. Make a buttonhole (or two, if you wish the straps to be adjustable) at the end of each strap and sew the buttons in place (see pages 15 and 16).

3. Hem the dress, either by overlocking the edge, pressing under 1cm (³⁄₈in) and stitching, or by pressing under a narrow double hem and stitching.

POMPOM TAIL

1. Draw a circle about 12cm (5in) on the cardboard. In the centre of this circle, draw a 4cm (1½in) circle. Cut out the ring shape from the cardboard. Repeat to create a second cardboard ring, and place the two rings on top of each other.

2. Cut several lengths of yarn, all the same length. Thread these repeatedly through the centre of the double-thickness ring, wrapping them around and around, and covering the ends as you go. Continue until you have a thick layer of yarn covering the cardboard ring all the way around.

3. Slip the scissor blade between the two layers of cardboard and cut through the yarn, working your way around the ring.

4. Wind a double length of yarn around the centre of the pompom, between the two cardboard rings, and tie it tightly.

5. Slide the cardboard rings off, and fluff up the pompom.

6. Hand sew the pompom in place at the back of the dress.

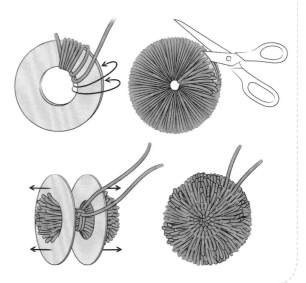

CAT & MOUSE DRESSES

Made here from cool, pure linen, this playful pair of dresses makes a perfect mix for sisters or best friends. Add bloomers to complete the outfit. The dress can be made with sleeves or without. I've added plain pink trims for the noses and ears but you could use pretty spots or ditsy florals – or substitute a rabbit face, using the template on page 210. The mouse dress is fully lined and the cat dress has a simple U-shaped neck facing, both with a keyhole back opening. The cat dress has a lovely tuck detail at the neckline, which adds detail to plain but special fabrics. I've topstitched this in a contrast thread for added detail.

YOU WILL NEED

A-line dress and cap sleeve patterns (follow the lines for a seamed shoulder, and with a tuck at the neckline as desired)

Mouse or cat templates

1 length of dress fabric for either dress (see Calculating fabric lengths, below)

Lining fabric, as required (or use self-fabric)

Contrast fabric for pockets, including contrast pocket binding, if desired

Fabric scraps in a suitable colour for nose, eyes and cat's or mouse's ears

Scraps of grey felt for mouse's claws

Iron-on, double-sided adhesive web

Button for back neck fastening

Tailor's chalk

Matching sewing thread

Contrast bright coloured sewing thread for the whiskers

CALCULATING FABRIC LENGTHS	6 MONTHS-3 YEARS	3-5 YEARS
Width 110cm (44in) dress	70cm (27½in)	1m (39in)
Width 150cm (60in) dress	70cm (27½in)	1m (39in)

(CON'T)

CUTTING OUT

NOTE: Seam allowances are 1cm (³⁄₈in) unless otherwise specified.

1. Choose the best size for your child, using the guide on page 26. Trace the pattern for the A-line dress available online (see page 11), (with or without the front neck tuck if you like) and for the Cat dress also trace the pattern for the cap sleeve available online, following the lines for the correct size. Make a pattern for the front, with the neck sitting lower, and another for the back.

2. Press the fabric and arrange it on a flat surface so you can cut out one dress front and one dress back piece. Make sure the centre front and the centre back are parallel to the selvedge.

3. Mark around the pattern pieces using tailor's chalk, adding 1cm (³⁄₈in) all around for seam allowances, and 2cm (³⁄₄in) at the hem. Cut out the pieces carefully. Cut two pairs of cap sleeves for the Cat dress. Cut pockets accordingly.

4. For the facings cut a U-shaped piece of fabric, as marked on the pattern, or follow the directions for a fully lined dress.

FACE & EARS

This requires some tricky sewing.

1. Using the mouse or cat templates on page 211, cut out four ears from self-fabric, adding 1cm (³⁄₈in) all around.

2. Bond adhesive web (see page 13) to the wrong side of the contrast fabric for the inner ears, nose and eyes. Trace the shapes on the backing paper, and cut out two inner ears, one nose, two eyes and six whiskers.

3. Mark the face position on to the dress with tailor's chalk.

4. Peeling off the backing paper, arrange the eyes, nose and whiskers on to the dress panel, and the inner ears on to the outer ears. Cover with a soft cloth and heat-press in place (see page 13). Using matching thread, topstitch around the edges. Create a cross shape through the eyes to make this easier, and a single line of stitching through the whiskers, taking care to backstitch at the start and finish of each whisker to secure.

5. Pin an outer ear front to an outer ear back, right sides together, and sew 5mm (¹⁄₄in) from the curved

edges. Snip into the curved seam allowances, turn through and press. Repeat to make a second ear.

6. Pin the ears in position to the face, with the ears pointing downwards and sew into position 5mm (¹⁄₄in) from the edge. Trim then press upwards and topstitch into place to create an ear that stands upward, but does move when the dress is worn.

MOUSE DRESS POCKETS

1. Overlock the edges of the pocket trim and press under 1cm (³⁄₈in) on all four edges. On the pocket, overlock the edges and then press under 2cm (³⁄₄in) on the top edge; topstitch. Press under 1cm (³⁄₈in) on the remaining edges. Pin the pockets to the right side of the dress front in the positions shown on the pattern.

2. Cut triangles of grey felt for the claws, each 4 × 2cm (1¹⁄₂ × ³⁄₄in). Insert three claws under the edge of each pocket, as shown.

3. Topstitch the pockets in place along the side and bottom edges, stitching 5mm (¹⁄₄in) from the edge, backstitching at the start and finish, and making sure the claws are caught in the stitching.

CAT DRESS SLEEVES

1. Using the cat template on page 211, cut out two ears from self-fabric, adding 1cm (³⁄₈in) all around, and two ears from contrast fabric.

2. Bond adhesive web (see page 13) to the wrong side of the contrast fabric for the nose and eyes. Trace the shapes on the backing paper and cut out.

3. Mark the face in position on to the sleeves with tailor's chalk.

4. Peeling off the backing paper, arrange the eyes and nose on to the sleeve. Cover with a soft cloth and heat-press in place. Using matching thread, topstitch around the edges. Create a cross shape through the eyes to make this easier.

5. For the whiskers, select a large straight stitch in a contrast colour and hand sew parallel lines to create whiskers that are 3mm (¹⁄₈in) apart, taking care to backstitch at the start and finish of each whisker to secure. Alternatively you may wish to use a satin stitch setting on your machine to do this.

(CON'T)

CAT DRESS POCKETS & NECK DETAIL

1. Cut two pockets from self-fabric, adding 2cm (¾in) to the top of the pocket only.

2. Prepare two bindings in contrasting colours that are long enough to wrap around the pocket edge. Refer to page 14 for more instructions on binding. Sew the binding around the edge of the pocket, leaving the top of the pocket open.

3. Overlock the top of the pocket, and press back 2cm (¾in) to create a finished edge.

4. Mark the pocket positions on the dress with tailor's chalk then position and pin into place.

5. Making sure the top of the pocket is folded back neatly, sew close to the edge of the binding and make a small backstitch across the top of the pocket to secure.

6. Create a tuck at the front neck if required. To do this, fold the front of the dress in half lengthways and sew 5cm (2in) down along the centre front line, backstitching to secure.

7. Press and sew the pleat into place using contrast thread – you can use the same thread as for the whiskers on the sleeve.

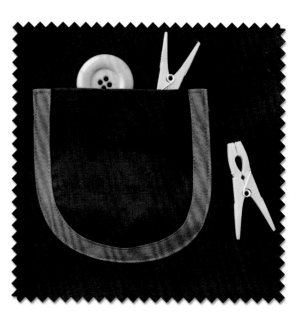

JOINING SLEEVES

1. For each of the two pairs of sleeves for the Cat dress, pin a main-fabric sleeve to a facing-fabric sleeve, right sides together, and sew along the outer curved edge.

2. Press the seam open and then fold back into place and press again. Sew the inner (lining-fabric) sleeve to the outer (main-fabric) one, wrong sides together, along the edge that will adjoin the body.

3. Pin the dress front to the dress back at the shoulders, right sides together, and sew the shoulder seams. Press the seams open.

4. Pin the sleeve in position around the armhole of the dress, right sides together, matching notches. Sew in place.

5. Overlock all remaining raw edges including the armholes and hem.

NECKLINE

1. Seam the U-shaped facing on the dress at the shoulders, right sides together. Pin it around the neckline. Mark the length of the back neck opening from the neckline down the centre back of the dress – about 8cm (3¼in). Pin around this mark.

2. Prepare a rouleau loop (see page 22) or take a short length of narrow ribbon, long enough to feed your chosen button through, plus 2cm (¾in). Fold the strip in half and pin into position, layered between the dress and the facing at the centre back point.

3. Using a small stitch setting, sew 5mm (¼in) all the way around the neckline, continuing around the keyhole opening. At the bottom of the opening, with the machine needle still in the fabric, release the machine foot, and pivot the fabric 180 degrees to sew back along the opposite side of the opening. Carefully trim the corners, turn the whole dress through and press. Topstitch edges as desired.

JOINING

Pin the side seams, right sides of the dress and right side of the facing together, carefully matching the armhole seams. On each side, sew in one continuous seam, 1cm (⅜in) from the edge. Press the seams open.

FINISHING

1. Finish the hem edge by turning 1cm (⅜in) under and stitching down. You can stitch the hem by hand if you prefer.

2. Topstitch carefully around the neck edge.

3. Turn under the overlocked underarm to the sleeve 5mm (¼in) from the edges, taking care at the curved edges.

4. Sew a button into place.

ROBIN CHARACTER DRESS

A great gift for the festive season, this cute winter dress has a generous pouch pocket for carrying precious things. You can also create a tropical bird by making the dress in brighter colours.

YOU WILL NEED

Character dress patterns: front, yoke, back facing, straps, breast panel and pouch pocket

Robin face templates

1 length of soft, medium-weight brown woven cotton, such as corduroy, velvet or cotton twill (see Calculating fabric lengths, below)

1 fat quarter of red fabric for pocket and breast panel

Beige felt scraps

Scraps of cotton fabric in orange and beige

Plain cotton or interfacing, as desired

30cm (12in) square of iron-on double-sided adhesive web

Elastic

2 buttons

Matching sewing thread

Tailor's chalk

CUTTING OUT

This unlined dress has a front yoke and shoulder straps, and is finished with front and back facings.

NOTE: Seam allowances are 1cm (³⁄₈in) unless otherwise specified.

1. Choose the best size for your child, using the guide on page 26. Trace the patterns for the Character dress available online (see page 11), following the lines for the correct size and including the side extensions for the dress back.

(CON'T)

CALCULATING FABRIC LENGTHS	6 MONTHS-3 YEARS	3-5 YEARS
110cm (44in)	1m (39in)	120cm (47in)
150cm (60in)	80cm (31½in)	1m (39in)

2. Press the main fabric and arrange it on a flat surface so you can cut out one dress front, one dress back, one back facing, two yokes and four straps. Make sure the grain lines on the pattern pieces are parallel to the selvedge and that any pile is running in the right direction.

3. Mark around the pattern pieces using tailor's chalk, adding 1cm (³/₈in) all around for seam allowances, and 2cm (³/₄in) at the hem. Cut out the pieces carefully.

4. Cut a large breast panel and pouch pocket from the red fabric, adding a 1cm (³/₈in) seam allowance.

5. If the yoke needs a little extra weight, cut another one from plain cotton or interfacing.

YOKE

1. Bond adhesive web to the wrong side of the orange and beige fabrics (see page 13). Using the robin face template on page 212, cut out one beak and two eyes.

2. Peeling off the backing paper, arrange the eyes and beak on the right side of one yoke. Cover with a cloth and heat-press. Stitch around the edges of the eyes and nose. If this is difficult, simply sew horizontal and then vertical lines to create cross shapes.

3. Pin this yoke to the other yoke, right sides together. Add interfacing to the wrong side of the front yoke if you wish. Pin the ears in place between the layers, with the raw edges even and the ear front next to the front yoke piece. Sew around the top curved edge of the yoke, 1cm (³/₈in) from the edge, trapping the ears in place as you go. Carefully snip the curved seam allowances, then turn through and press.

RED BREAST & POCKET

1. Press under 1cm (³/₈in) on the side and bottom edges. Pin right side up to the right side of the dress front in the position shown on the pattern, and topstitch around all the turned-under edges.

2. Using the template on page 212, cut strips of beige felt for the feet. Pin to the dress front in the position shown on the pattern, and stitch in place through the centre of each strip, backstitching to secure at each end.

3. Overlock the edges of the pocket and press under 2cm (³/₄in) on the top edge; topstitch. Using a safety pin, thread elastic through the channel you have created in the pocket, gather, and secure the elastic at the ends (see page 18).

4. Press under 1cm (³/₈in) on the remaining edges. Pin the pocket to the right side of the dress front in the position shown on the pattern. Topstitch in place along the side and bottom edges, stitching 5mm (¹/₄in) from the edge, backstitching at the start and finish.

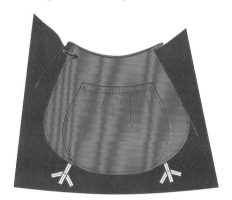

JOINING & STRAPS

1. Pin the dress front to the dress back at the side edges, right sides together. Sew the side seams, overlock the edges and press the seams towards the back.

2. To make a strap, pin two strap pieces with right sides together and sew around the edges with a 1cm (³/₈in) seam allowance, leaving the straight, narrow end open. Snip into the curved seam allowances, then turn through and press. Topstitch around the edges. Repeat to make the other strap. Sew the two straps in place at the shoulders on the dress back, right sides together and raw edges even.

3. Sew the two tucks on the right side of the dress front, with the tucks open towards the outer edges.

4. Pin the lower edge of the prepared yoke to the top edge of the dress front, right sides together. Stitch. Overlock the edges, turn back and press.

5. Overlock the lower, curved edge of the back facing.

6. Pin the back facing to the dress back around the outer edges, right sides together. Sew around the outer edges, trapping the shoulder straps as you go. Carefully snip the curved seam allowances and trim the corners. Turn through and press. Slipstitch the shorter facing edges to the dress side seams.

7. Topstitch 5mm (¹/₄in) from the edge all the way around.

FINISHING

1. Make a buttonhole (or two, if you wish the straps to be adjustable) at the end of each strap and sew the buttons in place (see pages 15 and 16).

2. Hem the dress, either by overlocking the edge, pressing under 1cm (³/₈in) and stitching, or by pressing under a narrow double hem and stitching.

CHEEKY MONKEY DUNGAREES

Here's a cheeky monkey overall for a mischievous little one. The classic character-dungaree shape can be used to create a whole host of critters, and using a good-weight soft fabric will make it warm and practical. It has been made here using heavy cotton corduroy, finished off with a perky polka-dot bandana.

YOU WILL NEED

Character dungaree, yoke, strap and pocket patterns

Monkey face templates

I length of medium-weight brown cotton, such as corduroy or cotton twill (see Calculating fabric lengths, below)

Beige fabric for face and inner ears

Contrast fabric for star and bottom patch

Fabric scraps for nose and eyes

Polka-dot fabric for bandana

Plain cotton or interfacing (optional)

30cm (12in) square of iron-on double-sided adhesive web

2 buttons

Matching sewing thread

Tailor's chalk

CUTTING OUT

SIZE GUIDE

Age	Height
6–18 months	up to 80cm (31½in)
18 months–3 years	up to 98cm (39in)
3–5 years	up to 110cm (44in)

These unlined dungarees have a front yoke and shoulder straps, and are finished with front and back facings.

NOTE: Seam allowances are 1cm (³⁄₈in) unless otherwise specified.

(CON'T)

CALCULATING FABRIC LENGTHS	6 MONTHS-3 YEARS	3-5 YEARS
110cm (44in)	120m (47in)	140cm (55in)
150cm (60in)	1m (39in)	120cm (47in)

1. Choose the best size for your child, using the guide on page 110. Trace the patterns for the dungarees available online (see page 11), following the lines for the correct size, the yoke and the turn-ups.

2. Press the main fabric and arrange it on a flat surface so you can cut out two dungaree fronts/backs, one yoke, two pockets and two straps. Make sure the grain lines on the pattern pieces are parallel to the selvedge and that any pile is running in the right direction.

3. Mark around the pattern pieces using tailor's chalk, adding 1cm (³/₈in) all around for seam allowances. Cut out the pieces carefully.

4. Using the dungaree pattern and adding 1cm (³/₈in) seam allowances all around, cut out the yoke facing, back facing, two straps and two turn-ups from contrast fabric.

5. If the yoke needs a little extra weight, cut another one from plain cotton or interfacing.

YOKE & BANDANA

1. Using the monkey face template on page 212, cut two pairs of ears from the main fabric, adding 1cm (³/₈in) all around.

2. Bond adhesive web (see page 13) to the wrong side of the fabric scraps and the beige fabric, for the face, features and inner ears. Using the monkey face template, mark the shapes on the backing paper and cut out the beige face and inner ears, and the eyes, nose and snout.

3. Peel off the backing paper from the beige face and position on the right side of the front yoke, adhesive side down. Cover with a soft cloth and heat-press. Stitch close to the edges. Attach the eyes, nose and snout to the face in the same way. Attach the inner ears to the main-fabric ears in the same way.

4. Pin an ear front to an ear back, right sides together, and sew 1cm (³/₈in) from the edge, leaving the bottom edge open. Carefully snip into the curved seam allowances. Turn through and press. Repeat for the second ear.

5. For the bandana, use the pattern available online (see page 11) to cut out two main bandana pieces and two smaller bandana pieces from the polka-dot fabric. Pin one to the other, right sides together, and stitch a 5mm (¼in) seam around the edge, leaving a small opening. Turn through and press, then sew

the opening closed. Sew to the face at the position shown on the pattern.

6. Pin this yoke to the other yoke, right sides together. Add interfacing to the wrong side of the front yoke if you wish. Pin the ears in place between the layers, with the raw edges even and the ear front next to the front yoke piece. Sew around the top curved edge of the yoke, 1cm (³/₈in) from the edge, trapping the ears in place as you go. Carefully snip into the curved seam allowances, then turn through and press.

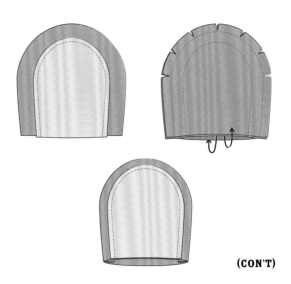

(CON'T)

POCKETS

1. Overlock the edges of the pockets. Add a star appliqué to a pocket if you wish, following the instructions in Yoke & bandana, steps 2–3.

2. Press under 2 cm (¾in) on the top edge of each pocket and topstitch. Press under 1 cm (⅜in) on the remaining edges.

3. Pin the pockets to the right side of the dungaree front in the positions shown on the pattern. Topstitch in place along the side and bottom edges, stitching 5mm (¼in) from the edge and backstitching at the start and finish.

BOTTOM PATCH

1. Trace the bottom-patch shape marked on the dungaree pattern, make a template for the shape, and use this to cut two bottom-patch panels from contrast fabric. Press under the curved edges.

2. Place a panel right side up on the right side of each dungaree back, at the position marked on the pattern. Topstitch close to the curved edge of each panel.

JOINING & STRAPS

1. Pin and stitch the two dungaree panels with right sides together at the centre front and centre back. It's worth stitching the centre back seam twice to make it extra hard-wearing. Overlock the seams and press towards the back.

2. Place one contrast turn-up strip along the hem edge with right sides together. Sew along the hemline, overlock and press open. Overlock the hem edge.

3. Pin and sew the inside leg seams, right sides together, from one hem to the other, including the turn-ups. Overlock the edges. Fold the turn-up under, pin and stitch it in place along the existing seam line. Repeat for the other turn-up.

4. To make a strap, pin two strap pieces with right sides together and sew around the edges with a 1cm (³⁄₈in) seam allowance, leaving the straight, narrow end open. Snip into the curved seam allowances, then turn through and press. Topstitch around the edges. Repeat to make the other strap. Sew the two straps in place at the shoulders on the dungaree back, right sides together and raw edges even, positioned so they will cross over the back when fastened.

5. Sew the two tucks on the right side of the dungaree front, with the tucks open towards the outer edges.

6. Pin the lower edge of the prepared yoke to the top edge of the dungaree front, right sides together. Stitch. Overlock the edges, turn back and press.

7. Overlock the lower, curved edge of the back facing.

8. Pin the back facing to the dungaree back around the outer edges, right sides together. Sew around the outer edges, trapping the shoulder straps as you go. Carefully snip the curved seam allowances and trim the corners. Turn through and press. Slipstitch the shorter facing edges to the dungaree side seams.

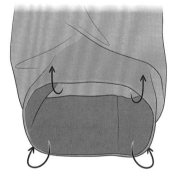

FINISHING

1. Topstitch 5mm (¹⁄₄in) from the edge all the way around.

2. Make a buttonhole (or two, if you wish the straps to be adjustable) at the end of each strap and sew the buttons in place on the back of the yoke (see pages 15 and 16).

SHARK DUNGAREES

This is the perfect overall for little boys and girls with a big sense of adventure. The padded fin on the back can be made soft enough for babies, too. Use a cotton moleskin, corduroy or cotton twill to withstand serious play!

YOU WILL NEED

Character dungaree, yoke, strap and pocket patterns

Shark face templates

Medium-weight grey cotton, such as corduroy or cotton twill (see Calculating fabric lengths, below)

Contrast fabric in red, white and black for mouth, teeth and eyes

Black fabric for fin and pockets approximately one fat quarter

Scraps of soft wadding or felt for inner fin

Interfacing (optional)

30cm (12in) square of iron-on double-sided adhesive web

2 buttons

Matching sewing thread

Tailor's chalk

CUTTING OUT

SIZE GUIDE	
Age	**Height**
6–18 months	up to 80cm (31½in)
18 months–3 years	up to 98cm (39in)
3–5 years	up to 110cm (44in)

These unlined dungarees have a front yoke and shoulder straps, and are finished with front and back facings.

NOTE: Seam allowances are 1cm (³⁄₈in) unless otherwise specified.

1. Choose the best size for your child, using the guide, left. Trace the patterns for the dungarees available online (see page 11), following the lines for the correct size, the yoke and the turn-ups.

(CON'T)

CALCULATING FABRIC LENGTHS	6 MONTHS–3 YEARS	3–5 YEARS
110cm (44in)	120m (47in)	140cm (55in)
150cm (60in)	1m (39in)	120cm (47in)

2. Press the main fabric and arrange it on a flat surface so you can cut out two dungaree fronts/backs, one yoke and two straps. Make sure the grain lines on the pattern pieces are parallel to the selvedge and that any pile is running in the right direction.

3. Mark around the pattern pieces using tailor's chalk, adding 1 cm (³/₈in) all around for seam allowances. Cut out the pieces carefully.

4. Using the dungaree pattern and adding 1 cm (³/₈in) seam allowances all around, cut out two pockets, one yoke facing, one back facing, two strap facings and two turn-ups from contrast fabric.

5. If the yoke needs a little extra weight, cut another yoke piece from plain cotton or interfacing.

YOKE

1. Bond adhesive web (see page 13) to the wrong side of the red, white and black scraps. Using the shark face template on page 211, mark the shapes on the backing paper and cut out the eyes from black, a mouth from red and teeth from white.

2. Peel off the backing paper from the pieces and position on the right side of the front yoke, adhesive side down, in the position shown on the pattern. Cover with a soft cloth and heat-press. Stitch close to the edges.

3. Pin this yoke to the other yoke, right sides together. Add interfacing to the wrong side of the front yoke, if you wish. Sew around the top curved edge of the yoke 1 cm (³/₈in) from the edge. Carefully snip into the curved seam allowances, then turn through and press.

POCKETS

1. Overlock the edges of the pockets. Press under 2 cm (³/₄in) on the top edge of each pocket and topstitch. Press under 1 cm (³/₈in) on the remaining edges.

2. Pin the pockets to the right side of the dungaree front in the positions shown on the pattern. Topstitch in place along the side and bottom edges, stitching 5mm (¹/₄in) from the edge and backstitch at the start and finish to secure.

FIN & BOTTOM PATCH

1. Using the fin pattern, cut out two fin pieces from black fabric and at least two inner fin pieces from the felt or wadding – use more for a fatter fin. Place the black fin pieces right sides together, and sandwich them between the inner fin pieces. Stitch along the seam line shown on the pattern, turn through and press.

2. Trace the bottom-patch shape marked on the dungaree pattern, make a template for the shape, and use this to cut two bottom-patch panels from contrast fabric. Press under the curved edges.

3. Place a panel right side up on the right side of each dungaree back, at the position marked on the pattern. Topstitch close to the curved edge of each panel.

(CON'T)

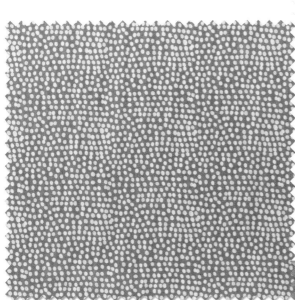

JOINING & STRAPS

1. Pin and stitch the two dungaree panels with right sides together at the centre front and centre back. Make sure you catch in the fin when stitching the centre back seam. It's worth stitching the centre back seam twice to make it extra hard-wearing. Overlock the seams and press towards the back.

2. Place one contrast turn-up strip along the hem edge with right sides together. Sew along the hemline, overlock and press open. Overlock the hem edge.

3. Pin and sew the inside leg seams, right sides together, from one hem to the other, including the turn-ups. Overlock the edges. Fold the turn-up under, pin and stitch it in place along the existing seam line. Repeat for the other turn-up.

4. To make a strap, pin two strap pieces with right sides together and sew around the edges with a 1 cm (³⁄₈in) seam allowance, leaving the straight, narrow end open. Snip into the curved seam allowances, then turn through and press. Topstitch around the

edges. Repeat to make the other strap. Sew the two straps in place at the shoulders on the dungaree back, right sides together and raw edges even, positioned so they will cross over the back when fastened.

5. Sew the two tucks on the right side of the dungaree front, with the tucks open towards the outer edges.

6. Pin the lower edge of the prepared yoke to the top edge of the dungaree front, right sides together. Stitch. Overlock the edges, turn back and press.

7. Overlock the lower, curved edge of the back facing.

8. Pin the back facing to the dungaree back around the outer edges, right sides together. Sew around the outer edges, trapping the shoulder straps as you go. Carefully snip the curved seam allowances and trim the corners. Turn through and press. Slipstitch the shorter facing edges to the dungaree side seams.

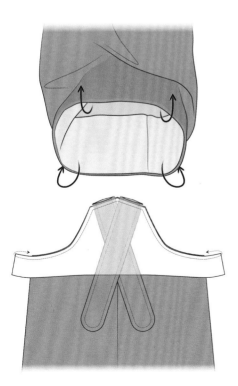

FINISHING

1. Topstitch 5mm (¹⁄₄in) from the edge all the way around.

2. Make a buttonhole (or two, if you wish the straps to be adjustable) at the end of each strap and sew the buttons in place on the back of the yoke (see pages 15 and 16).

TEDDY BEAR CHARACTER CAPE

This beautiful cape has a classic, lovable bear face. Made here in cotton velvet in an authentic toffee colour, it could also be done in chocolate brown for a fearsome grizzly bear, or in white for a beautiful polar bear. Perfect for dressing up and special parties.

YOU WILL NEED

Cape and character hood patterns

Bear face templates

120cm (47in) velvet or corduroy fabric, at least 110cm (44in) wide

120cm (47in) lining fabric, at least 110cm (44in) wide

Scraps of contrast fabric in cream and a dark shade of brown for inner ears, muzzle, nose and eyes

Iron-on double-sided adhesive web

1 button, 2cm (¾in) in diameter

Matching sewing thread

Tailor's chalk

CUTTING OUT

This hooded cape is fully lined and has hand openings in the front.

NOTE: Seam allowances are 1cm (⅜in) unless otherwise specified.

1. Choose the best size for your child, using the guide on page 26. Trace the patterns for the cape and character hood available online (see page 11), following the lines for the correct size. Make patterns for the cape front, back and side, and for the cape hood gusset, side panel and face panel.

2. Arrange the fabric on a flat surface so you can cut out two cape fronts, two cape sides, one cape back, one face panel, one hood gusset and two hood side panels from the main fabric. Make sure the grain lines on each piece are parallel to the selvedge.

3. Mark around the pattern pieces using tailor's chalk, adding 1cm (⅜in) all around for seam allowances. Cut out all the pieces carefully.

4. Repeat to cut out the same pieces from the lining fabric.

(CON'T)

FACE

1. Using the bear face template on page 213, cut out four inner ears from contrast fabric, adding 1cm (³⁄₈in) all around.

2. Bond adhesive web (see page 13) to the wrong side of the fabric for the inner ears, muzzle, nose and eyes. Trace the shapes on the backing paper, and cut out two inner ears, one muzzle, one nose and two eyes.

3. Peeling off the backing paper, arrange the eyes and muzzle on the face panel, the nose on the muzzle,

and the inner ears on the outer ears. Cover with a soft cloth and heat-press in place. Using matching thread, topstitch around the edges.

4. Pin an outer ear front to an outer ear back, right sides together, and sew 5mm (¼in) from the curved edges. Snip into the curved seam allowances, turn through and press. Repeat to make a second ear.

5. Pin the ears to the top of the face panel, with right sides together and raw edges even, at the positions marked. Stitch in place, referring to page 102, step 6.

HOOD

1. Pin the left and right hood sides to the gusset, right sides together, so the gusset is in the centre. Stitch both seams and press them open. Attach the top edge of the face to the front edge of the hood sides and gusset in the same way, right sides together.

2. Repeat step 1 for the hood lining.

3. Pin the main-fabric hood to the hood lining around the front edge, right sides together. Stitch around the front edge. Snip into the curved seam allowances, and turn through. Press, rolling the seam gently to obtain a good finish on the curved edges.

4. Topstitch 5mm (¼in) from the front edge.

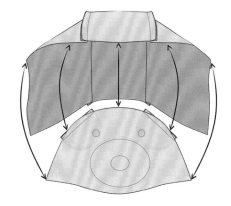

TIP
If you are using velvet, be sure to pin the seams first to ensure that they do not move as you sew – the pile of the fabric can cause movement. Always press gently on the reverse side, as too much pressure will damage the pile.

CAPE

1. From the main fabric, make a rouleau loop (see page 22) that is large enough to comfortably fit over the button you wish to use plus an additional 2cm (¾in) seam allowance.

2. Pin and stitch a cape side panel to each front panel, right sides together, leaving openings for the hands. Press the seams open.

3. Pin and stitch the side panels to the back panel, right sides together. Press the seams open.

4. Pin the lower edge of the hood to the cape neckline, right sides together, adding the rouleau loop to the right, so that it is sandwiched between the layers.

LINING

1. Make the cape lining in the same way as the main-fabric cape.

2. Pin the main fabric cape to the lining, right sides together. Sew all the way down the cape fronts and along the hemline.

3. Snip across the corners to give a neat finish, then pull the cape through the opening in the neck seam. Carefully press.

FINISHING

1. Position the armhole openings in the main cape and lining with wrong sides together and the seam allowances turned in, so that inner and outer pocket openings are aligned. Pin, then tack in place. Sew 5mm (¼in) from the edge of each opening.

2. Pin and topstitch 5mm (¼in) from the hand openings in the cape front, down both sides and across the top and bottom, through the main fabric and the lining.

3. Neatly stitch the opening in the hood neck seam closed.

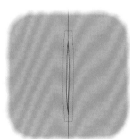

TOPS & BOTTOMS

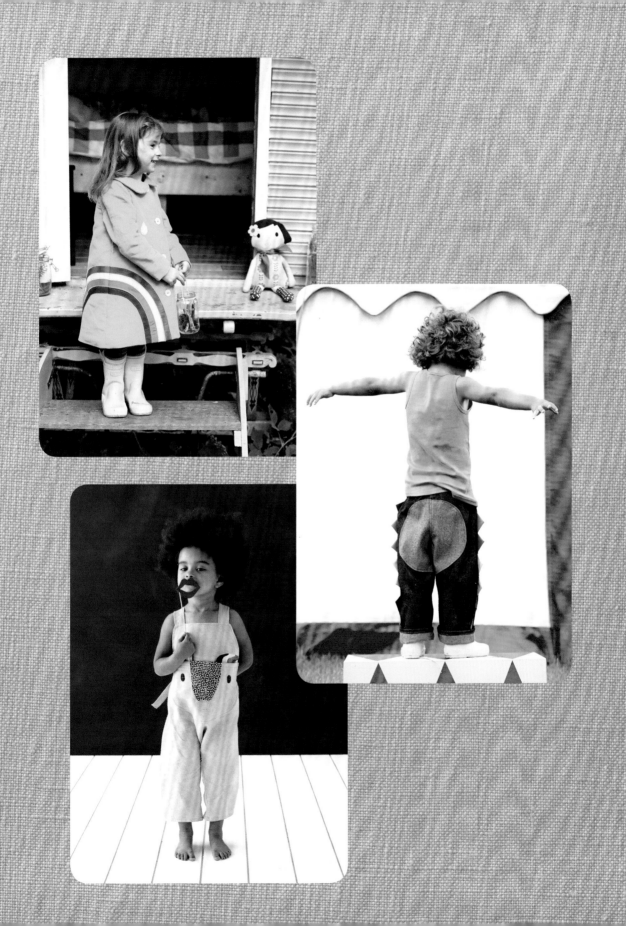

HIPPY CHICK FEATHER SUN TOP

This is a great festival top, especially for older girls. It can be cut to any length, for either a sun top or a sundress. The feathers are individually made and added to the neckline, so choose colours you like best. I've used rainbow shades, but simple white and gold or tonal combinations also work well.

YOU WILL NEED

Sun top pattern

Feather templates

75cm (30in) medium-weight print or plain fabric (I've used a medium-weight denim)

25cm (10in) or 1 fat quarter of self-fabric contrast cotton for binding and ties

Small fabric scraps in assorted colours, including some with metallic finish, for feathers

Iron-on double-sided adhesive web

Chunky beads in bright colours to decorate straps (optional)

Matching sewing thread

Tailor's chalk

CUTTING OUT

NOTE: Seam allowances are 1cm (⅜in) unless otherwise specified.

1. Choose the best size for your child, using the guide on page 26. Trace the pattern for the sun top available online (see page 11), following the lines for the correct size. Make a pattern for the front and another for the back.

2. Press the main fabric and arrange it on a flat surface so you can cut out a whole front and a whole back. Make sure the centre front and centre back are parallel to the selvedge and any pattern runs in the right direction.

3. Trace the pattern for the binding, following the lines for the correct size. Make a pattern for the binding.

5. Mark around the pattern pieces using tailor's chalk, adding 1cm (⅜in) all around for seam allowances on the front, back and yokes, and adding 2cm (¾in) at the hem on the front and back. Cut out the pieces carefully.

(CON'T)

ADDING DETAIL

1. For the feathers, bond adhesive web (see page 13) to the wrong side of the coloured fabric scraps. Peel off the backing paper, and bond to the wrong side of a different-coloured scrap. Using the templates on page 214, cut out about 30 feathers.

2. I have added an additional detail using gold and silver on the feathers, which can be added before the feather is cut out.

3. Stitch through the centre of each feather.

4. Pin the feathers to the top edges of the sun top front. Stitch close to the edge.

TIP
If you have some leftover bonded fabrics, use the feather pattern to make a feather headdress. You'll need a 6cm- (2¼in-) wide strip of felt long enough to fit around the child's head. Fold the felt strip in half lengthways, and insert the bottom of the feathers between the two halves; stitch in place along the top edge through both layers of felt and the feathers. Stitch a short piece of elastic to each end to make the band fit.

JOINING

1. Pin the dress front to the dress back at the side seams, right sides together. Stitch the seams; overlock.

2. Press under 1cm (³⁄₈in) twice on the hem; stitch.

3. Overlock the armhole edges, then turn under 5mm (¹⁄₄in) and stitch.

4. Bind the back and front neck edges following instructions on binding on page 14, turning the outer narrow edges inward to finish.

TIES

1. For the ties, press under 5mm (¼in) on each long edge and one narrow end of each of the strips, then fold in half lengthways and press. Stitch around the folded edges to create straps.

2. Sew each strap into place at the left and right corners, tucking the raw edge under before sewing. Alternatively, refer to the illustration below to make a simple pillowcase sun top.

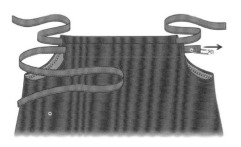

FINISHING

1. If desired, sew chunky beads onto the straps.

2. To fasten the dress, knot the straps at the shoulders.

PRINCESS CAPE

What little girl wouldn't want to wear a cape like this? An adaptation of the Red Riding Hood cape seen in my first book, this beautiful pixie-hooded play cape is made with a funky lining and jingle bells on the ties. The neck ties are made from fabric but you could substitute a decorative ribbon or braid if you prefer some sparkle.

YOU WILL NEED

Cape front, back and side, and hood patterns

120cm (47in) velvet or corduroy fabric, at least 110cm (44in) wide

120cm (47in) lining fabric, at least 110cm (44in) wide

Matching or contrast felt for tie trims

2 small jingle bells (available from most good haberdashery shops)

1 button, 2cm (¾in) in diameter (optional)

Rickrack trim (optional)

Matching sewing thread

Tailor's chalk

CUTTING OUT

This hooded cape is fully lined and has hand openings in the front.

NOTE: Seam allowances are 1cm (³⁄₈in) unless otherwise specified.

1. Choose the best size for your child, using the guide on page 26. Trace the patterns for the cape and character hood available online (see page 11), following the lines for the correct size. Make patterns for the cape front, back and side, and for the cape hood.

2. Arrange the fabric on a flat surface so you can cut out two cape fronts, two cape sides, one cape back and two hood panels, from the main fabric. Make sure the grain lines on each piece are parallel to the selvedge.

3. Mark around the pattern pieces using tailor's chalk, adding 1cm (³⁄₈in) all around for seam allowances. Cut out all the pieces carefully.

4. Repeat to cut out the same pieces from the lining fabric.

(CON'T)

TIES

1. For the ties, cut two 30 × 4cm (12 × 1½in) strips of lining fabric on the bias. On each, press under 1cm (³⁄₈in) on both long edges. Fold in half lengthways, then fold in 1cm (³⁄₈in) at one end. Stitch close to the turned-in edges.

2. Or, if you'd prefer to add a button, cut just one 10 × 4cm (4 × 1½in) bias strip and use it to create a fabric loop large enough for the button to fit through. Attach to the left-hand panel at the centre front neckline.

3. To make flower toggles for the ties from step 1, cut two 5cm (2in) felt flowers. Thread the end of each tie through the centre of the flower to form a stamen, and make a small knot. Add a bell to each for added magic!

HOOD

1. Pin the two main hood pieces with right sides together, and sew along the top and centre back. Trim the corner, and press. Repeat for the hood lining.

2. Pin the main-fabric hood to the lining hood around the front edge, right sides together; stitch. Press, turn through and press again.

3. If desired, sew rickrack trim on the right side of the hood, 2cm (³⁄₄in) from the front edge.

CAPE

1. Pin a cape side panel to each cape front panel, right sides together. Stitch, leaving openings for the hands. Press the seams open.

2. Pin and stitch the side panels to the back panel, right sides together. Press the seams open.

3. Right sides together, pin the lower edge of the hood to the cape neckline, adding a tie at the start and finish at centre front. Make sure the front edges of the hood and the cape align. Snip into the curved seam allowances and press the seam open.

LINING

1. Make the cape lining as for the Cape, steps 1–3; press. Pin the lower edge of the hood to the neck edge of the cape, right sides together. Stitch, leaving an opening at the back large enough to turn the cape through later. Press.

2. Pin the main-fabric cape to the lining, right sides together. Position the unstitched end of each tie at each side of the top front of the edge, right sides together and raw edges even. Sew all the way around, catching in the ties.

3. Snip across the corners to give a neat finish, then pull the cape through the opening in the neck seam. Carefully press.

FINISHING

1. Position the armhole openings in the main cape and lining with wrong sides together and the seam allowances turned in so that the inner and outer pocket openings are aligned. Pin then tack in place. Sew 5mm (¼in) from the edge of each opening.

2. Pin and topstitch 5mm (¼in) from the hand openings in the cape front, down both sides and across the top and bottom, through the main fabric and the lining.

3. Neatly stitch closed the opening in the hood neck seam.

4. If using a rouleau loop rather than a pair of ties, sew the button in place opposite the loop.

5. If desired, sew rickrack trim 2cm (¾in) above the hemline.

GO-FASTER SUPERHERO CAPE & CAP SET

Making this easy starter project will give you superhero status with the recipient. Choose favourite or team colours, or add a metallic trim. If you also add alternative decoration to the inside, the cape will be reversible for different roles. The cap makes a warm winter ear cover, too.

CAPE

YOU WILL NEED

Cape, panel and collar pattern

Star and lightning bolt templates

Assorted fabrics for panels, each 50cm (20in) long

Lining fabric, 50cm (20in) × full width of fabric

Scraps of contrast fabrics for decoration

30cm (12in) square of iron-on double-sided adhesive web

1 button, 2cm (¾in) in diameter or small square of sew-on hook-and-loop fastening

Matching sewing thread

Tailor's chalk

CUTTING OUT

This lined, circular cape consists of eight panels, topped with a collar constructed like a waistband.

NOTE: Seam allowances are 1cm (⅜in) unless otherwise specified.

1. Trace the pattern for the cape available online (see page 11), and make patterns for the panel and collar.

2. Press the fabrics and arrange them on a flat surface. Mark around the pattern pieces using tailor's chalk, adding 1cm (⅜in) all around for seam allowances. Make sure the grain lines on the pattern pieces are parallel to the selvedge.

3. Cut out eight panels and two collars.

4. Also cut out one full-size cape from lining fabric, adding a 1cm (⅜in) seam allowance all around.

(CON'T)

ASSEMBLY

1. Lay out the pieces in the correct sequence. Pin adjacent panels with right sides together along the long edges; stitch. Press the seams open.

2. Decide on the decoration for the back, using either the templates (see page 213) or your own design. Bond adhesive web to the scraps of contrast fabric (see page 13) and cut out the shapes.

3. Position the shapes, adhesive side down, on the right side of the cape at the back; heat-press into place. Topstitch close to the edges of the shapes.

4. Pin the lining to the cape, right sides together, along the lower and side edges. Stitch down one side edge, around the lower edge and up the other side edge.

5. Snip off the corners of the seam allowances, then turn through the neck opening. Press. Topstitch around the neck opening 5mm (¼in) from the edge.

COLLAR

1. Pin the two collar pieces with right sides together and stitch along the inner curved edge. Press the seam open. Press under 1cm (⅜in) on the outer curved edge of each piece and one end.

2. Unfold one side of the collar and pin its right side to the wrong side of the cape; stitch along the crease. (The tab extending beyond the side edge will be for the fastenings.) Press back.

3. Fold the collar over to the front and pin in place, concealing the seam. Topstitch along the fold 5mm (¼in) from the edge, continuing along the upper edge to complete.

FINISHING

Either add a buttonhole and button (see pages 15 and 16) at the opening, or sew the two halves of a square of hook-and-loop fastening in position so the cape will fasten.

CAP

YOU WILL NEED

Hat guesst and hat side patterns

Star template

I fat quarter or 30cm (12in) fabric

30cm (12in) lining fabric

Scraps of contrast fabric for piping, go-faster ears and decoration

30cm (12in) square of iron-on, double-sided adhesive web

I button, 2cm (¾in) in diameter, or small square of sew-on hook-and-loop fastening

Matching sewing thread

Tailor's chalk

▼▼▼▼▼▼▼▼▼▼

CUTTING OUT

SIZE GUIDE

Size	Age
XS	6 months
S	1–2 years
M	3–5 years
L	5–7 years

NOTE: Seam allowances are 1cm (³⁄₈in) unless otherwise specified.

1. Choose the best size for your child, using the guide, left. Trace the patterns for the hat gusset and hat side available online (see page 11), following the lines for the correct size.

2. Press the fabric and arrange it on a flat surface so you can cut out one gusset, one face panel and two sides. Make sure the grain lines on the pattern pieces are parallel to the selvedge and that any pile runs in the correct direction.

3. Repeat step 2 for the lining fabric.

4. Cut two go-faster panels from another contrast fabric.

5. Mark around the pattern pieces using tailor's chalk, adding 1cm (³⁄₈in) all around for seam allowances. Cut out the pieces carefully.

(CON'T)

ADDING DETAIL

1. Bond adhesive web to the wrong side of the fabric for the star (see page 13). Using the star template on page 213, cut two stars. Heat-press one into place on each side of the cap.

2. Cut two 45 × 3cm (18 × 1¼in) strips of contrast fabric on the bias. Fold in half lengthways and press. Pin one to each edge of the central gusset, right sides together. Secure by sewing 1cm (³⁄₈in) from the edge. Snip carefully into the gusset edge at regular intervals, so the cap will ease together during assembly.

3. For the first go-faster ear, fold over as shown on the pattern, and stitch 5mm (¼in) from the edges. Turn through, press, and repeat for the second ear.

Sew the ears in place on the top edge of the face panel, in the positions shown on the pattern.

TIP
If you choose a metallic finish, as I have, it's worth testing a scrap of the fabric before using it, as metallic finishes may tarnish or melt at high temperatures when bonding to adhesive web.

ASSEMBLY

1. Right sides together, pin the two side pieces to each side of the gusset, so the gusset is in the centre. Stitch the seams and press them open. Repeat for the lining.

2. Pin the outer hat to the lining, right sides together. Stitch all the way around, leaving an 8cm (3¼in) opening. Snip into the curved seam allowances and turn through.

3. Press, rolling the seam gently to obtain a good finish on the curved edges.

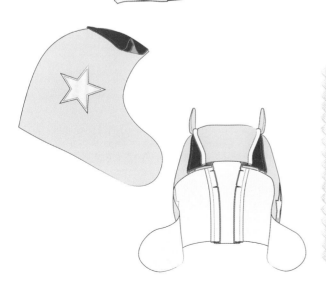

FINISHING

1. Topstitch 5mm (¼in) from the edge all the way around, closing the opening at the same time.

2. Either add a buttonhole and button at the opening, or sew the two halves of a square of hook-and-loop fastening in position so the cap will fasten.

QUILTED REVERSIBLE HOODED JACKET

This jacket for boys and girls uses a large-scale border print, which is lightly stitched through to quilt it, following the lines of the print design. It's great for any child, whether a baby or an older child. The cuffs turn back, making it easy to fit the sleeves. The edges are finished with a binding, which can be bought ready-made or made yourself.

YOU WILL NEED

Jacket front, back, sleeve, pocket and hood patterns

2 lengths of dress fabric, each 1m (40in) – choose one with an interesting border

Lining fabric for pockets

1m (39in) quilter's wadding (I've used a soft natural bamboo fibre wadding)

Bias binding – either home-made or ready-made, but ready-made will work better here

4 buttons, 2.5cm (1in) in diameter – or use poppers if preferred

Matching sewing thread

Tailor's chalk

CUTTING OUT

NOTE: Seam allowances are 1cm (³⁄₈in) unless otherwise specified.

1. Choose the best size for your child, using the guide on page 26. Trace the pattern for the jacket available online (see page 11), following the lines for the correct size. Make patterns for the front, back, sleeve, pockets and hood.

2. Press the fabric and arrange it on a flat surface so you can cut out one whole back, two fronts, two sleeves and hood pieces. Make sure the centre back and the grain line on the front pieces and sleeves are parallel to the selvedge. Take care to place the pattern over the most suitable part of the design if your design is large-scale. Depending on the design, it may be possible to match the pattern at the sides, so try to do this.

3. Mark around the pattern pieces using tailor's chalk, adding 1cm (³⁄₈in) all around for seam allowances, and 2cm (³⁄₄in) at the hem. Carefully cut out all the pieces.

4. Repeat steps 2 and 3 to cut out the lining and wadding.

(CON'T)

ADDING WADDING

1. For the outer main jacket back, sides, hood panels and sleeves, layer each piece in turn with the matching piece of wadding and sew all the way around the edges.

2. If your fabric has a pattern, you may wish to sew through the fabric and wadding, using a large stitch size, following the design pattern shape or line to add detail.

ASSEMBLING HOODS

1. Assemble the hoods left and right of the centre panel, according to the pattern.

2. Repeat for the lining.

3. Layer both hoods together and sew around the edges, ready to assemble to the main jacket.

POCKETS

1. Cut pockets from self-fabric, adding 2 cm (¾in) to the top of the pocket only.

2. Prepare bindings in contrasting colours that are long enough to wrap around the pocket edge. Refer to page 14 for more information on Binding. Sew the binding around the edge of the pocket, leaving the top of the pocket without.

3. Overlock the top of each pocket, and press back 2 cm (¾in) to create a finished edge.

4. Mark the pocket positions on the jacket with tailor's chalk, then position and pin into place.

5. Making sure the top of the pocket is folded back neatly, sew close to the edge of the binding to secure the pocket, making a small backstitch across the top to secure.

JOINING

1. Assemble the outer jacket. Pin the front to the back at the shoulders, right sides together, and stitch. Pin the sleeves into place, right sides together, and stitch.

2. Pin the side and underarm seams, right sides together, and stitch. Trim away the excess wadding from the seam allowances.

3. Repeat for the lining.

4. Assemble the hood along the neck edge to the main jacket.

5. Place the jacket lining right sides together at the neck edge and sew.

6. Now layer the entire jacket and sleeves together and sew along the outer edge and cuffs. Trim away excess fabric.

7. Bind the entire outer edge, starting at the hem at one of the side points and working your way around, via the neckline, front edges and lower edge, back to your starting point.

8. Bind the sleeve edges at the cuffs.

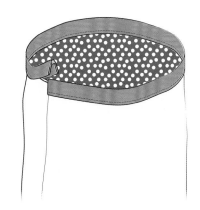

FINISHING

1. If using buttons, make buttonholes (see page 15) on the right front (for a girl) or the left front (for a boy). It would be a good idea to practise on layered fabrics first.

2. Mark the button position and sew a button to both front and back of the jacket (see page 16) to make it fully reversible.

LITTLE MISSY THEATRE COAT

Here's a special coat to wear for trips to the theatre – or for splashing in puddles! The coat pictured is fully lined, but it can be made unlined. Choose a coated fabric for weather-proofing on rainy days.

YOU WILL NEED

Coat front, back, collar, facing, sleeve and patch pocket patterns

Rainbow and raindrop templates

1m (39in) coat fabric

1m (39in) coat lining

Scraps of contrast fabric for the rainbow appliqué

Iron-on interfacing (optional)

30cm (12in) square of iron-on double-sided adhesive web

4 buttons, 2.5cm (1in) in diameter

Matching or contrast sewing thread

Tailor's chalk

CUTTING OUT

This A-line coat has long set-in sleeves, a button front and a Peter Pan collar, and is fully lined.

NOTE: Seam allowances are 1cm (³⁄₈in) unless otherwise specified.

1. Choose the best size for your child, using the guide on page 26. Trace the patterns for the coat available online (see page 11), following the lines for the correct size.

2. Press the fabric and arrange it on a flat surface so you can cut out one whole back, two fronts, two collars, two sleeves and one pocket. Make sure the centre back and the grain line on the pattern pieces are parallel to the selvedge.

3. Mark around the pattern pieces using tailor's chalk, adding 1cm (³⁄₈in) all around for seam allowances, and 2cm (¾in) at the hem. Carefully cut out all the pieces.

4. Repeat steps 2 and 3 to cut out the lining, omitting the collar and pocket.

POCKET

1. Overlock the pocket edges. Press under 2cm (¾in) on the top edge, and stitch. Press under 1cm (³⁄₈in) on the side and bottom edges.

2. Pin the pocket right side up on the right side of the coat front in the position shown on the pattern. Stitch 5mm (¼in) from the side and bottom edges, backstitching at the start and finish to secure.

(CON'T)

RIGHT-HAND SIDE SEAM & APPLIQUÉ

1. Pin the right-hand coat front to the back at the side edges, right sides together. Stitch the side seam and press the seam open.

2. Bond adhesive web to the wrong side of the contrast fabrics (see page 13). Using the rainbow template on page 215, draw the shapes on the right side of the fabric. Cut out the rainbow, numbering the stripes on the wrong side as you go. Cut out the raindrops.

3. Peel off the paper backing and arrange the pieces on the coat front, adhesive-side down. Take care to position the rainbow stripes accurately, so that when the side seam is sewn, they are correctly aligned. Cover the fabric with a cloth and heat-press the appliqué to bond the fabric.

4. Stitch around the edges of the pieces, using matching or contrast thread.

OTHER SEAMS

1. Pin the left-hand coat front to the other side edge of the back, right sides together. Stitch and press the seam open.

2. Pin and sew the sleeve underarm seams, right sides together. Press the seams open using a sleeve board if you have one.

3. Position each sleeve inside the armhole, right sides together, aligning the notches. Pin around the armhole, inserting the pins at a 90-degree angle to the edge of the fabric to help you ease the sleeve into the armhole. Stitch in place with the inside sleeve facing upwards.

COLLAR

1. It is unlikely that you'll need to strengthen the collar, as it is simply for decoration, but if you do, then press an iron-on interfacing to the wrong side of the collar facing.

2. Pin the two collar pieces with right sides together. Stitch around the curved outer edge of the collar.

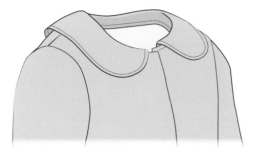

3. Snip into the curved seam allowances, and turn through. Press, then topstitch 5mm (¼in) from the outer edge.

4. Pin the fronts to the back of the coat at the shoulder seams, right sides together. Stitch the seams and press open. Repeat for the facings.

5. Pin the collar in place around the neckline, right sides together, between the notches as marked on the pattern. This is to make an overlap or button stand at the front so that once closed, the collar edges meet and don't overlap. Stitch the neckline seam.

6. Press the hem edge back by 4cm (1½in). To create a tailored finish, you may wish to add a strip of interfacing to the inside turn-back. If you do, cut to 3cm (1¼in) wide to create a tailored finish.

LINING

1. Add interfacing to the front facing if required, by cutting this to the same size as the facing pattern, minus seam allowances.

2. Sew the facing to the lining front, right sides together. Sew the lining side seams and sleeves into position. Instead of ease at the sleeve, you can simply add a small tuck.

3. Place the main-fabric coat and lining with right sides together. Pin around the neckline, front edges and lower edge. Stitch, press the seams open and trim the corners. Turn through.

FINISHING

1. Press thoroughly. (Pressing throughout is so important to achieve a professional result.) Do it carefully, making sure you don't over-press and damage the fabric, especially if it has a nap or pile.

2. Topstitch 5mm (¼in) from the outer edge, all the way around.

3. Secure the turned-back hem at the side seams by sewing discreetly through the layers with a small tacking stitch.

4. Finish the sleeves by pressing under 4cm (1½in) and slipstitching the lining – turned back by 1cm (⅜in) – into place inside.

5. Carefully make 4 buttonholes that run horizontally to the centre front, on the right side of the coat (see page 16). Mark then sew the buttons into place.

BAT HOODIE

With its superhero mask on the hood, this hoodie makes a perfect instant dressing-up outfit. I've used a silver fabric for the goggles on the hood's top panel, but bright colours would work well for them, too, and you could also have contrast colours on the ears and wings. The hoodie uses fleece fabric, requiring a stretch stitch.

YOU WILL NEED

Hoodie front and back, sleeve, pocket, batwing, hood side and gusset, and face panel patterns

Superhero mask and wing templates

1m (39in) sweatshirt fabric or fleece, at least 110cm (44in) wide

Contrast fabric for mask

Contrast jersey fabric for hood lining (or use the main fabric)

Iron-on double-sided adhesive web

Matching and contrast sewing thread

Tailor's chalk

CUTTING OUT

This hoodie has an unlined body with long sleeves and a lined hood.

NOTE: Seam allowances are 1cm (³⁄₈in) unless otherwise specified. For this project, set your machine to a suitable stretch stitch, as recommended in your machine manual.

1. Choose the best size for your child, using the guide on page 26. Trace the pattern for the hoodie available online (see page 11), following the lines for the correct size. Make patterns for the hoodie front, with the neck sitting lower and the bottom edge straight, and another for the back, with the lower curved bottom edge. Also trace the patterns for the hoodie sleeve, pocket, batwing, hood side, hood gusset and face panel.

2. Press the fabric and arrange it on a flat surface so you can cut out one front, one back, two sleeves, one pocket, four batwings, two hood sides, one hood gusset and one face panel. If you are using the main fabric to line the hood, then the face panel can be cut with the fabric folded to eliminate the seam at the hood edge. Make sure the centre back and the grain line on the pattern pieces are parallel to the selvedge.

3. Mark around the pattern pieces using tailor's chalk, adding 1cm (³⁄₈in) all around for seam allowances, and 3cm (1¼in) at the hem of the front, back and sleeves. Carefully cut out all the pieces.

4. From the lining fabric, cut two hood sides, one gusset and one face.

(CON'T)

APPLIQUÉ

1. Fold the face panel along the lines marked on the pattern, to create a double semi-circular panel. Alternatively, seam the face panel with the matching lining piece along the straight edge and fold back.

2. Bond adhesive web to the wrong side of the contrast fabric (see page 13). Using the superhero mask template on page 209, trace around the shape onto the backing paper, and cut out.

3. Peeling off the backing paper, position the mask on the face panel. Heat-press using a moderate iron.

4. Topstitch close to the edge of the mask.

5. Using the template on page 209, cut two ears from the main fabric. Pin the straight edges of each with right sides together, and stitch a narrow seam to create two cone shapes. Snip off the point of each seam allowance and turn through. Sew the ears in place on the face panel at the positions indicated on the pattern.

6. Following the pattern, repeat for the colour inlay of the wings.

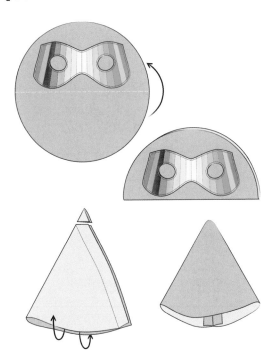

HOOD

1. Pin the left and right hood sides to the gusset, right sides together, so the gusset is in the centre. Stitch both seams and press them open. Repeat for the hood lining.

2. Place the main-fabric hood and the hood lining right sides together, with raw edges even. Pin the curved edge of the face panel between the layers, around the curved front edge of the hood. Stitch the seam. Keeping the face panel out of the way, continue to sew the outer edges of the hood together, but leave an opening at the back edge. Turn through the opening and press.

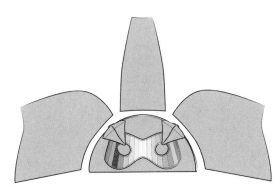

POCKET

1. Overlock the edges of the pocket. Press under 2cm (¾in) on the two edges for the hand openings, and stitch. Press under 1cm (⅜in) on the remaining sides of the pocket.

2. Pin the pocket right side up on the right side of the hoodie front at the position marked on the pattern. Topstitch in place close to the top edge and the lower, curved edge, backstitching at the ends.

WINGS

1. With right sides together, pin one pair of wing pieces along the outer edge; stitch. Snip off the points within the seam allowances, turn through and press. Repeat to make the other wing.

2. Topstitch the outer edge, and topstitch along the lines indicated on the pattern, using contrast thread if preferred.

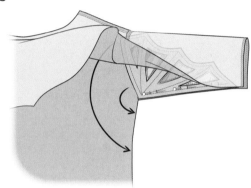

JOINING

1. Pin the front to the back at the shoulders, right sides together. Stitch the shoulder seams. Overlock and press.

2. Pin each sleeve to the hoodie front and back, right sides together. Stitch the seams.

3. Overlock each lower sleeve edge.

4. With right sides together and raw edges even, pin one underarm and side seam from the lower edge of the sleeve to the lower edge of the hoodie, sandwiching the wing between the two layers. Stitch the underarm and side seam as one continuous seam. Overlock and press. Repeat for the other underarm seam.

5. Overlock the lower hem edge, then press under 3cm (1¼in) and stitch. Press.

6. Press under 3cm (1¼in) on the lower edge of each sleeve and stitch. Press.

7. Pin the lined hood to the hoodie front and back around the neck, right sides together, overlapping the front corners of the hood slightly at centre front. Stitch the seam. Overlock and turn through.

DOGHOUSE SWEATSHIRT

This cosy but funky sweatshirt for boys and girls is made from stretch fabric, so it is perfect for everyday play. Choose a contrast geometric or polka-dot fabric for the ears. If preferred, incorporate a different character face featured in this book.

YOU WILL NEED

Raglan sweatshirt top front, bottom front, back, sleeve, pocket and neck band patterns

1m (39in) sweatshirt fabric or fleece, at least 110cm (44in) wide

Contrast fabric scraps for the ears and features

Contrast sweatshirt fabric or fleece for pockets and neck welt (you can use the reverse side of the main fabric if preferred)

Iron-on double-sided adhesive web

Matching sewing thread

Tailor's chalk

CUTTING OUT

NOTE: Seam allowances are 1cm (³⁄₈in) unless otherwise specified. For this project, set your machine to a suitable stretch stitch, as recommended in your machine manual. A straight stitch is feasible, however you may wish to gently extend the stretch of your fabric as you sew to create a seam which itself has some stretch to it, to avoid the seams cracking when worn.

1. Choose the best size for your child, using the guide on page 26. Trace the patterns for the raglan sweatshirt in the envelope, following the lines for the correct size.

2. Press the fabric and arrange it on a flat surface so you can cut out one top front, one bottom front, one back and two sleeves. Make sure the centre back, centre front and grain line on the pattern pieces are parallel to the selvedge.

3. Mark around the pattern pieces using tailor's chalk, adding 1cm (³⁄₈in) all around for seam allowances, and 3cm (1¼in) at the hem of the bottom front, back and sleeves. Carefully cut out all the pieces.

4. From the main fabric or contrast fabric, cut out two pockets and a neck band, adding the same 1cm (³⁄₈in) seam allowance except for the pocket opening, where you will need to add 2cm (³⁄₄in).

(CON'T)

TIP
To make a sweatshirt incorporating a cat face, use the face and ears from the cat dress on page 100, enlarging the template first to 125 per cent. The star appliqué here could be replaced by a small silver bell on a narrow ribbon, sewn into the horizontal seam.

APPLIQUÉ

1. Bond adhesive web to the wrong side of the contrast fabric (see page 13). Using the dog templates on page 214, trace around the shapes onto the backing paper, and cut out.

2. Peeling off the backing paper, position the shapes on the top front. Heat-press using a moderate iron. Topstitch close to the edges of the shapes.

3. Using the dog template on page 214 and adding 1 cm (³⁄₈in) all around for seam allowances, cut two ears from the main fabric (for the ear backs) and two from the contrast fabric (for the ear fronts).

4. Pin an ear front to an ear back, right sides together, and stitch around the outer edge, leaving the straight end unstitched. Snip into the curved seam allowances, turn through and press. Repeat for the second ear.

5. Pin each ear to the right side of the top front at the position shown on the pattern, with the printed ear front facing outwards.

POCKETS

1. Overlock the edges of the pockets. Press under 2 cm (³⁄₄in) on the top edge and topstitch in place. Press under 1 cm (³⁄₈in) on the remaining pocket edges.

2. Pin each pocket, right side up, to the right side of the bottom front at the positions shown on the pattern. Topstitch close to the side and bottom edges, backstitching at the start and finish.

JOINING

1. Pin the lower edge of the top front to the upper edge of the bottom front, right sides together. Stitch and then press the seam.

2. Arrange the body and sleeve pieces ready to sew. Sew the sleeves in place to the front of the garment, right sides together to create the front raglan. Sew the sleeves in place to the back of the garment, right sides together to create the back raglan. Overlock the seams and press.

3. Overlock the lower cuff edges of the sleeves.

4. With the sweatshirt folded with right sides together, sew the side seams and underarm seams as one continuous seam. Overlock and press.

5. Overlock the hem edge, then press under 3cm (1¼in) and stitch in place. Press.

6. Press under 3cm (1¼in) on the overlocked lower edge of the sleeves. Stitch.

7. Pin one end of the neck band to the other end, right sides together, and stitch a 1cm (³⁄₈in) seam. Press the seam open.

8. Fold the neck band in half lengthways, wrong sides together. Tack the raw edges together. Pin the neck band around the neck edge, right sides together and raw edges even, easing it to fit. Stitch in place. Press the band away from the front and back pieces, and the seam allowance towards the front and back pieces.

REVERSIBLE KITTY TODDLER TROUSERS

These reversible trousers are really practical and great for little crawlers on the move. The bottom patch makes a lovely detail and also adds a layer of durability. The trousers can be made extra warm by using heavier fabrics. You could also adapt the cat template to other animals, such as a panda, or whatever your child fancies.

YOU WILL NEED

Dungarees pattern

Cat ear, inner ear and paw templates

75cm (30in) length of each of 2 contrast fabrics

Scraps of plain fabrics in contrast colours for eyes, nose and paws

30in (12in) square of iron-on double-sided adhesive web

60cm (24in) length of 2cm- (¾in-) wide elastic

Heavy embroidery thread

Matching or contrast sewing thread

Tailor's chalk

CUTTING OUT

This reversible trouser is elasticated at the waist.

NOTE: Seam allowances are 1cm (³⁄₈in) unless otherwise specified.

1. Choose the best size for your child, using the guide, right. Trace the pattern for the dungarees available online (see page 11), following the lines for the correct size and the trouser line. Make a pattern for half of the front/back.

2. Press both pieces of fabric, arrange on a flat surface and fold in half so that the selvedges meet. You could place one on top of the other, aligning the folds, to cut out both at once. Place the patterns on the fabric, making sure the grain lines are parallel to the selvedge.

3. Mark around the pattern pieces using tailor's chalk, adding 1cm (³⁄₈in) all around for seam allowances. Carefully cut out a left front/back and a right front/back from each of the two fabrics.

SIZE GUIDE

Age	Height
6–18 months	up to 80cm (31½in)
18 months–3 years	up to 98cm (39in)
3–5 years	up to 110cm (44in)

(CON'T)

EARS

1. Using the ear template on page 214, cut four ears from the contrast fabric for the face and ear.

2. Bond adhesive web (see page 13) to the wrong side of the contrast fabric for the inner ears. Using the inner-ear template on page 214, cut out two inner ears.

3. Peel off the backing paper and bond the inner ears to the right side of two of the ears. Using matching thread, topstitch the inner ears 2mm from the edges.

4. Pin one of the ears from step 3 to one of the other two ears, right sides together. Sew 5mm (¼in) from the side edges, leaving the bottom edge open. Trim a small triangle shape from the tip of the ear, close to the seam, to give a neat, pointed finish. Turn through and press from the wrong side. Topstitch close to the side edges. Repeat with the remaining two pieces to make the other ear.

BOTTOM PATCH & CAT FACE

1. Trace the bottom-patch shape marked on the dungaree pattern, make a template for the shape, and use this to cut two bottom-patch panels from contrast fabric, adding 1cm (³⁄₈in) all around. Press under the curved edges. It is useful to use the paper pattern piece as a template for the curve so that you fold the edges and press around the template itself to achieve a smooth curve.

2. Place a panel right side up on the right side of each trouser back, at the position marked on the pattern.

3. Insert an ear under each patch in the position shown on the pattern, so the bottom edge of each ear will be caught in the seam, and the ears project beyond the face, with the inner ears on top. Topstitch close to the curved edge of each panel.

4. Bond adhesive web (see page 13) to the wrong side of the contrast fabric scraps for the eyes and nose.

5. Peel off the backing paper, cover with a cloth and heat-press the nose and eyes to the face in the positions indicated. Stitch close to the edges. If this gets difficult, you can simply sew horizontally, then vertically, to create a cross shape.

6. Using tailor's chalk, mark the whiskers on the face and embroider as lines of straight stitches, using a heavy embroidery thread and an embroidery needle.

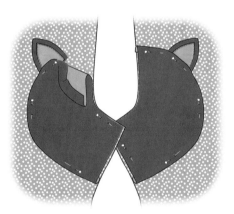

PAWS

1. Bond adhesive web (see page 13) to the wrong side of the paw fabric, using contrast colours if preferred. Using the templates on page 214, cut out two sets of paws.

2. Peel off the backing paper from the paws, cover with a cloth and heat-press to the knees in the positions shown on the pattern. Stitch close to the edge of each paw, as for the nose and eyes (step 5).

JOINING

1. Pin and stitch the two trouser panels in one fabric with right sides together at the centre front and centre back. It's worth stitching the centre back seam twice to make it extra hard-wearing. Overlock the seams and press towards the back. Repeat for the two trouser panels in the other fabric.

2. Pin and sew the inside leg seams, right sides together, on both pairs of trousers.

3. Turn one pair of trousers through, and place inside the other pair, so they are right sides together. Pin and sew the two pairs together around the waistline.

4. Turn the trousers through to the right sides, through one of the legs. Press to give a neat finish at the waist.

5. Stitch 2.5cm (1in) from the top edge to create a channel for the elastic.

6. Measure your child's waist (or see the guide on page 26) and deduct 5cm (2in); cut a length of elastic to this length. Using a safety pin, thread the elastic through the channel, stitch the elastic to the waist at each end to secure, and then sew the opening closed. After you've arranged the gathers, it's a good idea to backstitch the sides several times to stop the elastic from rolling.

7. Press under the hems on the bottom edge so the trousers are the same length, and then sew the hems on each leg together, 5mm (¼in) from the edge.

DINO BUNTING TROUSERS

This style works well for boys and girls and looks stunning with a simple T-shirt that picks up one of the colours in the bunting detail at the side seams. I've used denim for the trousers, and the reverse side of the denim for the bottom patch, which matches the turn-ups. The seat patch makes the trousers extra durable, while the bunting could also be used as a great border detail for dresses and skirts.

YOU WILL NEED

Dungaree pattern
(follow the lines for
the trouser)

75cm (30in) length of
fabric, or 50cm (20in)
for size 6–18 months

Contrast fabric for
bottom patch
(or reverse side of denim, if
using denim as main fabric)

Fabric scraps in contrast
colours for bunting

60cm (24in) length of
2cm- (¾in-) wide elastic

Heavy embroidery thread

Matching or contrast
sewing thread

Tailor's chalk

CUTTING OUT

These trousers have side seams, centre front and centre back seams and an elasticated waist.

NOTE: Seam allowances are 1cm (³⁄₈in) unless otherwise specified.

SIZE GUIDE

Age	Height
6–18 months	up to 80cm (31½in)
18 months–3 years	up to 98cm (39in)
3–5 years	up to 110cm (44in)

1. Choose the best size for your child, using the guide, left. Trace the pattern for the dungarees (with a side seam) available online (see page 11), following the lines for the correct size and the trouser line. Make a pattern for the front and another for the back.

2. Press the fabric and arrange it on a flat surface so you can cut out two fronts and two backs. Place the patterns on the fabric, making sure the centre front lines are parallel to the selvedge.

3. Mark around the pattern pieces using tailor's chalk, adding 1cm (³⁄₈in) all around for seam allowances. Carefully cut out two fronts and two backs.

(CON'T)

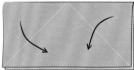
BUNTING

1. From the contrast fabrics, cut out fourteen 10cm (4in) squares (or smaller for smaller trouser sizes).

2. Fold each square in half and press. Now fold the two corners that are on the fold towards the opposite raw edges, so the folds meet in the middle and you have a triangle shape. Press again.

3. With raw edges even and the side with the central fold against the right side of the trouser front, pin a bunting piece to the side edge of the trouser front. Repeat for the remaining bunting pieces along the side seams, spacing equally. Allow sufficient space at the hem edge to make a hem.

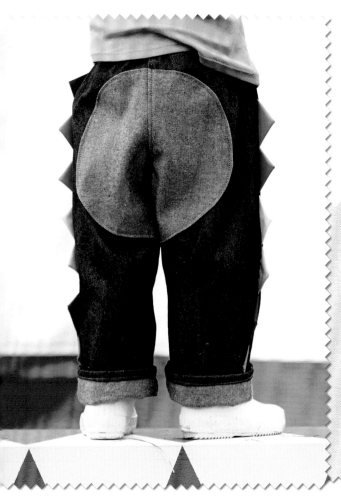

BOTTOM PATCH

1. Trace the bottom patch shape marked on the dungaree pattern, make a template for the shape, and use this to cut two bottom patch panels from contrast fabric, adding 1cm (3/8in) all around. Press under the curved edges. It is useful to use the paper pattern piece as a template for the curve so that you fold the edges and press around the template itself to achieve a smooth curve.

2. Place a panel right side up on the right side of each trouser back, at the position marked on the pattern. Topstitch close to the curved edge of each panel.

JOINING

1. Right sides together, pin the front trouser to the back trouser along the side seams, with the bunting sandwiched between the two layers. Stitch the side seams and overlock.

2. Now assemble the two halves. Pin and stitch the centre front and centre back seams of each half, right sides together; it's worth stitching the centre back seam twice to make it extra hard-wearing. Overlock the seams and press the seam back.

3. Pin and sew the inside leg seam, right sides together; overlock.

4. Stitch 2.5cm (1in) from the top edge to create a channel for the elastic.

5. Measure your child's waist (or see the guide on page 26) and deduct 5cm (2in); cut a length of elastic to this length. Using a safety pin, thread the elastic through the channel, stitch the elastic to the waist at each end to secure, and then sew the opening

closed. After you've arranged the gathers, it's a good idea to backstitch the sides several times to stop the elastic from rolling.

6. Press under 5mm (¼in) twice on the lower edge cuff of each leg. Stitch to form a hem, working with the inside of the leg facing upwards to enable you to manoeuvre the hem easily when sewing.

BABY HAREM DUNGAREE

This has to be one of my favourites. Its easy-to-wear contemporary shape is great for little boys and girls. Made here in linen, this style looks good in denim, too. The crossover apron back looks lovely on its own in the summertime. Choose bright and funky fabrics for the ears and snout. You can also interchange the face or the pocket with others in this book.

YOU WILL NEED

Apron dungaree front and back, bib facing and pouch pocket patterns

Baby harem dungarees templates

1m (39in) medium-weight plain fabric, such as denim, corduroy, linen or canvas

20 × 17cm (8 × 7in) rectangle of contrast fabric for nose and bottom patch

Scraps of plain fabric in contrast colours for eyes and nose

Iron-on double-sided adhesive web

About 30cm (12in) length of 2cm- (¾in-) wide elastic

20cm (8in) length of 1cm- (⅜in-) wide cotton tape (or use self-fabric)

Matching or contrast sewing thread

Tailor's chalk

CUTTING OUT

These unlined dungarees are finished with a bib facing at the front. The straps cross over at the back, where they are tied.

NOTE: Seam allowances are 1cm (⅜in) unless otherwise specified.

1. Choose the best size for your child, using the guide on page 26. Trace and make the patterns for the apron dungaree front and back, bib facing, and accompanying pocket available online (see page 11), following the lines for the correct size.

2. Press the main fabric and arrange it on a flat surface so you can cut out one whole front, one whole back and one bib facing. Make sure the centre

front and centre back are parallel to the selvedge. If you are using linen, be careful, as the fabric can 'move' when cutting.

3. Mark around the front and back pattern pieces using tailor's chalk, adding 1cm (¾in) all around for seam allowances, and 3cm (1¼in) at the hem and the waist back. Mark around the bib facing pattern piece, adding 1cm (¾in) all around for seam allowances. Cut out the pieces carefully.

4. Using the pocket pattern, cut one patch pocket from the main fabric with a 1cm (⅜in) seam allowance all around and 3cm (1¼in) to the top edge of the pocket.

(CON'T)

POCKET

1. Using the pattern available online (see page 11), cut out one snout from the contrast fabric. Turn under the edges, except for the top (straight) edge. Topstitch it in position on the pocket.

2. Bond adhesive web (see page 13) to the wrong side of the contrast fabrics you have chosen for the eyes and nose. Using the templates on page 214, cut out two eyes and one nose from these fabrics.

3. Overlock the edges of the pocket.

4. Arrange the eyes and nose in position on the pocket. Cover with a cloth and heat-press in place (see page 13). Using matching or contrast thread, stitch around the edge of the nose, and stitch each eye with two straight lines in a cross shape.

5. Press under 2.5cm (1in) on the top edge of the pocket; stitch. Press under 1cm (³/₈in) on the remaining edges.

6. Using the template on page 214, cut two ears from plain fabric and two from a striped fabric. Pin a plain ear to a striped ear, right sides together. Sew 5mm (¹/₄in) from the edges, leaving the bottom edge open. Turn through and press from the wrong side. Repeat with the remaining two pieces to make the other ear.

7. Position the pocket on the front of the dungarees. Pin in place and topstitch 2mm from the side and bottom edges, backstitching at the start and finish.

8. Pin the ears to the dungarees behind the pocket at the positions shown on the pattern, so they are pointing downwards into the pocket. Stitch in place. Now press the ears upwards along the stitching, and stitch again. This will seal the raw edges and allow the ears to stay upright.

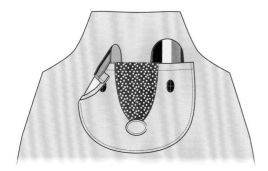

STRAPS

1. Cut two 85 × 7.5in (33 × 3cm) strips from the main fabric.

2. Press under 1cm (³/₈in) on both long edges and one end of each strap. Fold in half lengthways and press again.

3. Pin and stitch down the long edge and across the end.

BOTTOM PATCH

1. Using the bottom-patch pattern, cut one bottom patch from contrast fabric, adding 1cm (³/₈in) seam allowance all around.

2. Press under the curved edge. Place right side up on the right side of the dungaree back, at the position marked on the pattern.

3. Topstitch close to the curved edge of each panel.

JOINING

1. On the top edge of the dungaree back, press under 1cm (³/₈in) and then a further 2.5cm (1in). Stitch in place.

2. Using a safety pin, thread the elastic through the channel created in step 1. The approximate length will be 20cm (8in) for size 6 months–2 years, 23cm (9in) for size 3–4 years, or 25cm (10in) for size 5–6 years. Smooth out the gathers and secure the elastic at each end by stitching through all layers.

3. Pin the dungaree front to the back, right sides together, at the sides. Sew both side seams, and overlock the edges.

4. Pin a strap to each top corner of the bib on the right side, with the raw edges even.

5. Cut the length of tape or strip of self-fabric into two 10cm (4in) lengths. Fold each in half to form a loop, and sew in place on the dungaree front at the positions shown on the pattern.

6. Pin the bib facing to the dungaree front, right sides together, then sew around the edge. If you are using a heavy fabric, snip away the corners of the seam allowances to reduce bulk when turned through. Turn through so that the bib facing is on the inside. Press.

7. Overlock the lower edge of the bib facing.

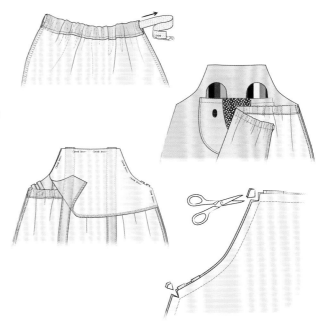

FINISHING

1. Topstitch the top and side edges, 5mm (¹/₄in) from the edge.

2. Press under 5mm (¹/₄in) twice on the lower edge of each leg; stitch.

3. Secure the bib facing on the inside by slipstitching.

4. To wear, cross the shoulder straps at the back, take them through the loops and then tie in a bow.

LAYERED PARTY SKIRT

This classic skirt is perfect for a border-printed fabric, for which there are many beautiful designs available. Adding a layer of tulle over the top, or using it as a lining, will give extra twirl and bounce. I've also added a ruffle to the underskirt for an extra touch of drama.

YOU WILL NEED

50cm (20in) fabric, either 110cm (44in) or 150cm (60in) wide for the outer skirt

50cm (20in) fabric, either 110cm (44in) or 150cm (60in) wide for the underskirt

10cm- (4in-) wide strip, the full width of the fabric, which either matches or contrasts with the underskirt

Additional 50cm (20in) fabric, either 110cm (44in) or 150cm (60in) wide for the added ruffle (optional)

Iron-on double-sided adhesive webbing or interfacing (optional)

Matching sewing thread

Tailor's chalk

Note: No pattern is required for this style. If you are using a border print that runs along the selvedge of the skirt, allow about 75cm (30in) if the border is at both edges, or 150cm (60in) if it is not.

CUTTING OUT

NOTE: Seam allowances are 1cm (³⁄₈in) unless otherwise specified.

1. Decide on the length of the skirt and add 3cm (1¼in) for the hem and waistband allowance. Cut the underskirt to this length across the full width of the fabric, making sure the grain line is parallel to the selvedge.

2. Cut the outer skirt to the length of the underskirt minus 6.5cm (2½in), again making sure the grain line is parallel to the selvedge.

3. The waistband is already to scale. If the fabric is lightweight, you may wish to strengthen it by heat-pressing (see page 13) an 8cm- (3¼in-) wide strip of iron-on adhesive webbing or interfacing to the waistband. (Do not interface the seam allowances of the waistband.)

(CON'T)

PREPARING & GATHERING THE SKIRT

1. Overlock all the edges of both skirts.

2. Place the outer skirt on top of the underskirt, both right side up. Gather the top edge (see page 18) of both layers together. Take your time so you don't snap the threads.

ADDING THE RUFFLE (OPTIONAL)

1. Cut three or four strips, full width of the fabric and 6cm (2 ¼in) deep. Seam these together, overlock then hem.

2. Gather the raw edges so that they are equal to the measurement of your skirt lining hem. This will take time, so be patient, and take care not to snap the gathering threads.

3. Place the gathered ruffle right sides facing to the hem edge of the lining.

4. Seam the ruffle to create a continuous band. Sew into place. Overlock.

ADDING THE WAISTBAND

1. Press under 1cm (³⁄₈in) on all edges of the waistband strip, then press in half lengthways.

2. Measure your child's waist, and mark a length equal to this measurement on the waistband, with equal amounts beyond the marks.

3. Unfold one long edge of the waistband. With raw edges even, pin the right side of the waistband to the wrong side of the underskirt along this unfolded waistband edge. Stitch in place, then press the seam upwards into the waistband.

4. Fold the waistband over to the front. Pin and stitch the folded waistband edge in place, covering the previous stitching. Continue sewing all the way along the waistband ties at each side, and also along the tips of the ties.

JOINING

1. Pin the side edges of the underskirt with right sides together. Mark a point on the side edges 8cm (3¼in) from the top. Stitch the side seam from the bottom to the marked point. Press the seam open, continuing to press the seam allowances on the unstitched portion all the way to the top.

2. Repeat step 1 for the overskirt, stopping the stitching at exactly the same distance from the top.

3. Press under 2cm (¾in) at the hem of each skirt.

ACCESSORIES & PLAYTIME

RUFFLE KNICKERS

These little baby knickers make a perfect gift and can be made to coordinate with a sun top or a shortened A-line dress. They are also gorgeous on their own, so why not incorporate plenty of ruffles in a rainbow design? They make a good nappy cover – to cover cloth nappies, make them a size bigger and use a water-resistant fabric layer inside.

YOU WILL NEED

Knickers pattern

25cm (10in) or 1 fat quarter of fabric

4cm- (1½in-) wide bias-cut strips for ruffles

About 1m (39in) of 5mm- (¼in) wide elastic (see Calculating elastic lengths, below)

Matching sewing thread

Tailor's chalk

CUTTING OUT

These unlined knickers have an elasticated waist and legs.

NOTE: Seam allowances are 1cm (⅜in) unless otherwise specified.

1. Choose the best size for your child, using the guide below. Trace the pattern for the knickers available online (see page 11), following the lines for the correct size.

2. Press the fabric and lay it on a flat surface. Mark around the pattern pieces using tailor's chalk, adding 1cm (¾in) all around for seam allowances. Cut out a knicker front and a knicker back.

(CON'T)

CALCULATING ELASTIC LENGTHS	6 MONTHS-18 MONTHS	18 MONTHS-3 YEARS
Waist	44cm (17½in)	27cm (10½in)
Leg	48cm (19in)	30cm (12in)

RUFFLES

1. Referring to the pattern, mark the ruffle positions on the knicker back with tailor's chalk.

2. Gather each ruffle (see page 18). You will need roughly three times the length to create a generous ruffle.

3. Pin each ruffle, right side up, on the right side of the knicker back, trimming each ruffle to length.

4. Topstitch down the centre of each ruffle.

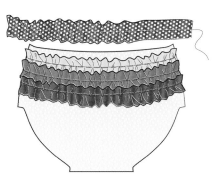

ELASTICATING THE LEGS & ASSEMBLING

1. Place the knicker front and back pieces right sides facing and sew the side seams.

2. Overlock these seams, and the entire leg opening on both sides.

3. Sew the gusset seam together and overlock.

4. Prepare two cut lengths of narrow elastic according to the size you have used, as indicated on the pattern. Join these at one end by sewing together carefully so that you have an elastic loop.

5. To add this to the knicker leg edge, turn back each leg edge by 1 cm (^{3}/8in) trapping the elastic inside the channel, and sew all the way around, as shown in the illustration. Take care not to sew into the elastic itself so that the elastic finally runs freely within the channel you have created.

ANIMAL HAT

This faux fur hat makes a perfect winter hat, with cosy ear warmers, as well as a great dress-up piece. A nod to Maurice Sendak's favourite classic *Where The Wild Things Are*, your child will love wearing this whatever the weather. You can also increase the sizes to make an adult hat if you like.

YOU WILL NEED

Hat pattern

25cm (10in) faux fur fabric, approximately 50 × 70cm (20 × 27in)

Lining fabric (same size as faux fur fabric), either printed or plain cotton, or an old soft t-shirt

Contrast funky print for the inner ears and ear warmers

Matching sewing thread

Tailor's chalk (optional)

A pointed implement, such as a bradawl or small scissors to tease trapped fur

CUTTING OUT

1. Prepare the pattern to the correct size by measuring your child's head circumference and using the guide below. Cut out the pattern for the crown, head circumference main, ears and ear warmers. For adult sizes, adapt the length of the top circle pattern and sides accordingly.

SIZE GUIDE

Age	Height
6–24 months	51cm (20in)
2–4 years	54cm (21in)
4–7 years	56cm (22in)

2. Trace the pattern for the animal hat available online (see page 11), following the lines for the correct size.

3. Smooth the pile of fabric in one direction. Lay the pattern on reverse of fabric and mark in tailor's chalk, adding 1cm ($^3/_8$in) to the edges as seam allowance.

4. Cut one hat main and circular crown piece, two ears and two ear warmers.

5. Repeat by cutting a hat main and circular crown piece in the lining fabric.

6. Cut two inner ears and two inner ear warmers in the contrast funky print.

(CON'T)

EARS & EAR WARMERS

1. Place each printed ear inner and outer right sides together, sewing around the edges with a 1 cm (³/₈in) seam allowance.

2. Snip the point and turn through. Use a pointed implement such as a bradawl to tease trapped fur strands from the seams.

3. Repeat steps 1 and 2 above for the ear warmers.

JOINING

1. Starting with the crown, snip out triangular shapes as marked, cutting to the point shown. Fold the circle in two, inserting the ears into place. Sew.

2. Construct the main part of the hat by sewing into a cylindrical shape.

3. Place the crown in place, pinning it first and making sure that the front, back and sides are aligned to the markers. As faux fur can be bulky, stay tacking can help.

4. Repeat steps 1–3 for the lining, leaving a small opening of approximately 7.5cm (3in) around the crown through which you will later bag or turn the hat through.

5. Place the ear warmers into position at the sides of the main hat, equally spaced, and sew into position.

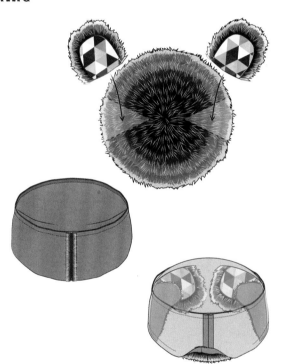

FINISHING

1. Place the outer fabric and lining right sides together, and pin along the hat edge.

2. Sew the fabric and lining together.

3. Pull to the right side through the opening you have left in the lining.

4. Sew this opening either by machine or hand to finish.

5. Use a pointed implement to tease trapped fur strands from the seams.

LITTLE LION SLIPPERS

A lovely baby gift and a great way to upcycle scraps, these slippers are made from fabric and felt but could be made from scraps of soft leather if you're feeling adventurous (see page 185). However, do make sure that whatever you use is non-hazardous to babies, who love to chew their toes. You can also try another character, such as a cat, using the template on page 211. The slippers are based on a design I made for my son, Ewan, which he treasures today.

YOU WILL NEED

Slipper pattern

Slipper templates

Fabric for slipper toe fronts, backs and soles

Polka-dot fabric for lining

Scraps of felt or contrast fabric in orange for the mane and ears

Contrast fabric for the nose and eyes

Iron-on adhesive web

Lightweight wadding (or felt if you prefer a softer, less lightweight slipper)

Narrow elastic

Small piece of 1cm- (³⁄₈in) wide cotton tape

Matching or contrast sewing thread

Tailor's chalk

CUTTING OUT

NOTE: Seam allowances are 5mm (¼in) unless otherwise specified.

Each fabric slipper is made from a sole, a back and an embroidered front that has a stitched-on felt mane and ears, and the three pieces are padded and lined prior to being sewn together.

1. Trace the pattern for the slippers available online (see page 11). Make a pattern for the front, another for the back and another for the sole.

2. Mark around the pattern pieces using tailor's chalk, adding 1cm (³⁄₈in) all around and taking care to mark the notches. From the scraps of main fabric, carefully cut out one front, one back and one sole for each shoe.

3. Cut out the same pieces from the polka-dot lining fabric and also from the wadding or felt.

4. Using the pattern, and adding a 5mm (¼in) seam allowance for each slipper, cut out 16 small felt circles (or contrast orange fabric) for the lion's mane and four small felt circles for the lion's ears. You may alternatively wish to cut your felt circles for the mane without seam allowance and use them with the straight cut edge of the felt for ease.

(CON'T)

LION'S FACE & MANE

1. Bond adhesive web (see page 13) to the wrong side of the contrast fabric for the eyes and nose. Using the pattern, trace around the template to cut out two eyes and a nose for each slipper.

2. Peel off the backing paper and bond the eyes and nose into place. Finish by topstitching down with matching thread, 2mm from the edges. Mark and sew whiskers into place with either a satin stitch or parallel straight stitch lines.

3. Prepare the mane and ear pieces. Take two orange semicircles, place them right sides together and sew 5mm (¼in) from the edge. Turn through and press. For the ears, repeat with one side in orange and the other side in the spot fabric.

4. Arrange the mane. Pin three circles for the mane to the top edge of one slipper front, right sides facing, then overlap with two circles for the ears in the correct position. Sew in place 5mm (¼in) from the edge. Repeat for the other slipper.

ASSEMBLING

1. Pin a small tab of cotton tape to the right side of each lining front at the centre of the straight edge, turning under the ends of the tape and stitching it in place. This will be used as a channel through which the elastic will be threaded.

2. Assemble the front toe pieces. For each slipper, place the lining front and the slipper front with right sides together, and place the wadding front on the wrong side of the lining. Stitch 5mm (¼in) from the edge, leaving an opening. Turn through and press, and stitch the opening closed.

3. To assemble the back pieces, pin a lining back to each main-fabric back, right sides together, then layer a piece of wadding to this. Stitch 5mm (¼in) along the longer edge, leaving the short end open. Turn under 1cm (³⁄₈in) at the shorter end and press. Now stitch 1.5cm (⁵⁄₈in) from the longer edge to create a channel, sewing around the narrower end to seal.

4. Pin a lining sole to each main-fabric sole, right sides together, then place the wadding sole in between. Stitch 5mm (¼in) from the edge, leaving an opening. Turn through and press, and stitch the opening closed.

JOINING

1. With right sides together and matching the notches, pin the toe front into place on the sole. Sew 1cm (³⁄₈in) from the edge.

2. Pin the slipper back to the remainder of the edge of the sole, working from the centre back to the front, right sides together, 1cm (³⁄₈in) from the edge. The back and top pieces should overlap.

3. Overlock neatly or use a machine satin stitch (refer to your machine manual) to finish the raw edges. Turn through.

FINISHING

1. Using a safety pin, thread the elastic cut to size according to the pattern through the channel in the slipper back.

2. Adjust the elastic to the required length, stitch the channel closed and feed the raw edges of the elastic back through the channel to hide them.

TIP
If you use leather for the slippers, you will need no lining – only the outer slipper. To make a channel for the elastic, cut a 1cm- (³⁄₈in-) wide strip of the leather to the length of the top of the heel section, and stitch in place.

ANIMAL EARS CUSHION

This jolly cushion makes a great gift and it can be created in any size. Try making it super-sized as a giant floor cushion, or smaller to fill with barley or lavender. The instructions here are for making the two cushions pictured but you could easily adapt them to make a different face.

YOU WILL NEED

Face templates

Fabric for cushion cover

Contrast fabric for ears, snout, eyes and whiskers

Rectangular or square cushion pad to desired size

30cm (12in) square of iron-on double-sided adhesive web

1 button, 2cm (¾in) in diameter (optional)

Embroidery thread in assorted colours (optional)

Matching sewing thread

Tailor's chalk

CUTTING OUT

This rectangular cushion has an envelope (overlap) opening at the back.

NOTE: Seam allowances are 1cm (³⁄₈in) unless otherwise specified.

1. Measure the length and width of your cushion pad and deduct from each measurement: 6cm (2¼in) if it is large, 4cm (1½in) if it is medium-sized, or 2.5cm (1in) if it is small. Make a pattern to these dimensions, to give a plumper cushion than if the cover were made to the full size of the cushion pad.

2. Mark a solid line down the centre of the pattern, and a dotted line parallel to it and two-thirds of the way from one side edge to the other.

3. Press the fabric and arrange it on a flat surface. Using the whole pattern, cut out one front, adding a 1cm (³⁄₈in) seam allowance all around. Now fold the pattern along the dotted line, so it is two-thirds the size of before, and cut out two backs, adding a 1cm (³⁄₈in) seam allowance alongside the folded edge of the pattern.

4. Unfold the pattern. Using the face templates on pages 210 and 214, mark the design onto the reverse side of the pattern, and trace off the relevant shapes. Cut out one snout and four triangular or rabbit ears from the contrast fabric, adding a 1cm (³⁄₈in) seam allowance all around.

(CON'T)

ADDING THE FACE

1. Turn under 1 cm (³⁄₈in) on the snout and pin it to the front. Topstitch in place close to the edge.

2. Bond adhesive web (see page 13) to the wrong side of the fabric scraps for the other features. Using the templates on pages 210 and 214, mark the shapes on the backing paper and cut out the features; for each of the two cushions shown here, you need two eyes and one nose, and for the rabbit face you also need two inner rabbit ears and six whiskers (unless you prefer to embroider them – see step 6).

3. Peel off the backing paper and arrange the snout, eyes and whiskers (if using) on the right side of the front, adhesive side down. Cover with a soft cloth and heat-press (see page 13). Topstitch around the edges of the eyes and snout to secure. If this gets difficult, you can simply sew straight lines horizontally, then vertically, to create a cross shape.

4. If you are including rabbit ears, peel the backing paper off the adhesive web and position the inner ears, adhesive side down, on the right side of two ear pieces, as shown on the template. Heat-press then topstitch 2mm from the edges.

5. Whether you are including rabbit ears or triangular ears, pin the two ear fronts to the two ear backs, right sides together, and sew 1 cm (³⁄₈in) from the edges, leaving them open at the bottom edge. Trim a small triangle shape at the tip of the ear, close to the seam, to give a neat, pointed finish, and snip into any curved seam allowances. Turn through and press from the reverse side. You can topstitch 2mm from the edges if you wish. If desired, sew a small tuck into the base of each rabbit ear to make the ear more rigid. Pin the ears to the cushion cover front, with raw edges even and the front ear against the right side of the cushion cover front.

6. If you wish to embroider the whiskers rather than appliqué them, use a contrasting colour of embroidery thread and an embroidery needle to embroider lines of backstitch or running stitch extending out from the snout. You could also embroider other features if you wish, such as a mouth or eyebrows.

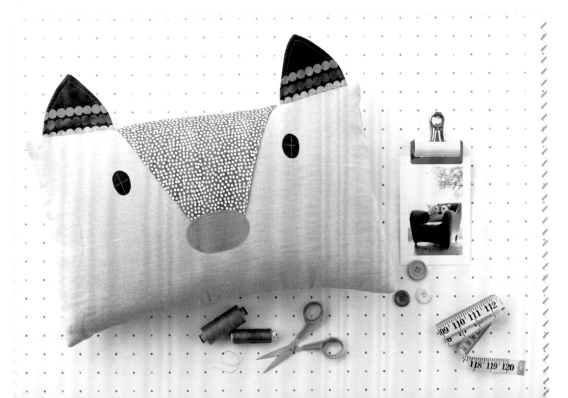

JOINING

1. Press under 2cm (¾in) twice on the left-hand side edge of one back piece and the right-hand side edge of the other back piece.

2. With the hemmed edges on the back pieces overlapping, pin the two back pieces to the front piece, right sides together and raw edges even. Stitch all the way around the edges, trapping the ears in the seam.

3. Overlock the raw edges.

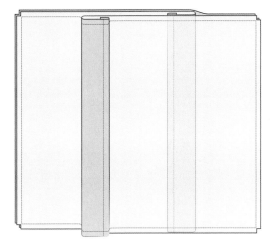

FINISHING

1. If desired, make a buttonhole in the middle of the overlapping hemmed edge on the back, and sew a button on the underlap to correspond (see pages 15 and 16).

2. Insert the cushion pad through the opening and fasten the button if using.

TIP
To add lavender or barley, create a small square pouch from a scrap of fabric, so that this can be removed from time to time from the cushion.

SUNSHINE STORAGE PLAY MAT

This clever smiling sun doubles as a play mat for a baby or a toy transporter for a toddler. It can also be used as a sleep quilt for either age. Made from a generous 120cm (47in) circle of fabric, it forms a cheerful play area when flat, or a colourful flower to hold toys, especially blocks, when the drawstring is pulled up.

YOU WILL NEED

Play mat face and bunting templates

Two pieces of canvas, each 120cm (47in) square

Ten 25cm (10in) squares of fabric in assorted colours, for bunting

Scraps of contrast fabric, for face

30cm (12in) square of iron-on double-sided adhesive web

Quilter's wadding

1m (39in) fabric, for bias binding

Heavy cotton cord

Matching sewing thread

Tailor's chalk

String, pencil and pin or drawing pin

CUTTING OUT

This circular play mat consists of two layers of canvas, with wadding between them. Resembling piping, the binding around the edges actually forms a casing for a drawstring.

NOTE: Seam allowances are 1cm (³/₈in) unless otherwise specified.

1. To make a pattern for a 120cm (47in) circle, tie a pencil to a piece of string and secure the other end of the string with a pin or drawing pin, adjusting the length until the pencil will be exactly 60cm (24in)

from the pin when the string is taut. Stick the pin securely at the centre of a large piece of paper and draw the circle (or a quarter-circle if you prefer).

2. Press the two pieces of canvas. Using tailor's chalk, draw around the edge of the pattern onto one fabric square (or, if using a quarter-circle pattern, move the pattern as necessary to draw all four quarters, forming a circle). Sandwich the wadding square between the two squares of canvas, with the marked circle on top, and pin around the edge. Cut out the circle from all three layers at once.

(CON'T)

APPLIQUÉ

1. Bond adhesive web (see page 13) to the wrong side of the fabrics for the features. Enlarge the templates on page 216 to a size appropriate for the size of play mat you are making, and mark the shapes on the backing paper. Cut out two eyes, two cheeks and one smiling mouth.

2. Peel off the backing paper and arrange the eyes, cheeks and mouth on the right side of the top canvas circle, adhesive side down. Cover with a soft cloth and heat-press (see page 13). Topstitch close to the edges to secure.

3. Pin the top canvas circle (with the face), right side up, to the wadding and, beneath that, the other canvas circle (the base). Pin around the edge through all three layers; stitch.

> **TIP**
> Why not create a second design on the base of the mat? You could use templates from the book, such as the rainbow template on page 215, and enlarge the scale as necessary.

BUNTING

1. Cut brightly coloured bunting for the edges each measuring 30 × 17 cm (12 × 6¾in). Prepare by seaming down the centre back of each piece and pressing into shape. Arrange around the edges of the mat and sew into place.

2. Trim away any excess.

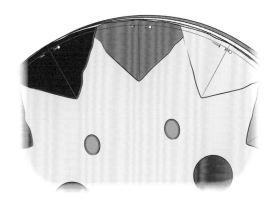

BINDING

1. Cut 3m (118in) of 14cm- (5½in-) wide strips on the bias. Join the ends (see page 14). Press under the long edges by 1cm (⅜in), then fold in half lengthways and press.

2. With the canvas base still on top, open out the binding, turn back the end by 5mm (¼in). Pin the binding around the edges through all the layers (binding, bunting, canvas base, wadding and canvas top), right sides together and raw edges even. Stitch along the pressed fold, 1cm (⅜in) from the raw edge. Continue all the way around, taking care not to pull too tightly. As you get back to the starting point, turn back the end of the binding by 1cm (⅜in), wrong sides together, trimming off the excess binding, and ending about 2cm (¾in) short of the starting point.

3. Fold the binding over to the canvas top. With the pressed edge turned under, pin in place all around, and topstitch in place, covering the previous stitching. Take your time to do this accurately.

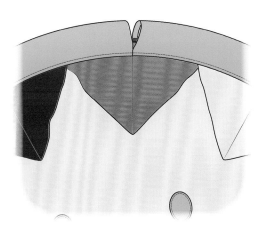

FINISHING

1. Using a safety pin, insert the cord through the opening and into the channel formed by the binding.

2. Tie knots in the ends of the cord to stop it from disappearing inside the channel. Pull up the cord to use the play mat for storage.

PARTY TEPEE

Create a special hideaway for your little ones, giving them 'me space' and a place to read, play or take a nap. Incorporating some of my signature graphic appliqués, it makes a colourful addition to a playroom, is perfect in the garden and is easy to roll away for storage. Add bright cushions inside to make it even more appealing. The bold colours make the tepee perfect for boys and girls, especially siblings who share rooms.

YOU WILL NEED

Tepee patterns: side panel, lower front and upper front

Balloon templates

4m (157½in) plain fabric

Fabrics in rainbow colours, for balloon appliqué and flags

Eight 25cm (10in) squares of fabric in assorted colours, for bunting

Stiff fusible interfacing, for flags (optional)

Iron-on double-sided adhesive web

20cm (8in) elastic

1.6m (1¾yd) ready-made bias binding for the bunting

Narrow ribbon for the balloon strings, approximately 3m (118in)

Rainbow ribbon for the bow

50cm (20in) webbing tape (optional)

4 wooden dowels, each 175cm (69in) long

4 rubber feet for dowels (optional)

4 buttons

Fine-grade sandpaper (optional)

Matching or contrasting sewing thread

Tailor's chalk

CUTTING OUT

This tepee has a 1m- (39in-) square base, and the sides are 140cm (55in) long, making the tepee 165cm (65in) high overall. The front is divided into an upper panel and two doors beneath it. The underlying structure consists of four dowels that run along the seams joining the panels and are joined at the top, projecting beyond the fabric cover. There is also a separate 1m- (39in-) square mat.

NOTE: Seam allowances are 1cm (³⁄₈in) unless otherwise specified.

1. Use the pattern available online (see page 11), using the specified amount and make patterns for a side panel, a lower front and an upper front. Enlarge to scale. You may wish to work directly on to the fabric with tailor's chalk to avoid excess paper usage. Press the fabric and arrange it on a flat surface so you can cut out three sides, two lower fronts and one upper front. Make sure the grain line is parallel to the selvedge.

2. Mark around the pattern pieces using tailor's chalk, adding 1cm (³⁄₈in) for seam allowances but 5cm (2in) on the opening edge of each lower front. Cut out the pieces.

(CON'T)

3. On the three side panels and the upper front panel, trim 5cm (2in) from the top of each point.

4. From the same fabric, cut eight 20 × 12cm (8 × 5in) rectangles for the dowel channels, four 60 × 6cm (24 × 2¼in) strips for the doorway ties, and a 104cm (41in) square for the mat.

APPLIQUÉ

1. Bond adhesive web to the wrong side of each piece of fabric for the sun and the balloons (see page 13). Using the template on page 209, draw the shapes on the front of the fabric using tailor's chalk, and cut out.

2. Peel off the backing paper and centre the sun and its rays, adhesive side down, on the right side of the lower edge of the upper front panel. Cover with a soft cloth and heat-press in place.

3. Topstitch close to the edges, using matching or contrast sewing thread.

4. Repeat steps 1 and 2 for the balloons, positioning the two halves of each very carefully on the side and lower front panels.

ASSEMBLY

1. To make the doorway, press under 1cm (³⁄₈in) and then a further 3cm (1¼in) on the opening edge of each lower front panel; stitch. With the two lower front panels right side up and overlapping at the narrow end by 1cm (³⁄₈in), pin or tack them together. Lay the upper front panel on top, right sides together and with the lower edge of the upper panel even with the upper edges of the lower panels. Pin and stitch along this edge. Overlock.

2. Pin each front panel to a side panel along the long edges, right sides together, taking care to match the rainbow stripes. Stitch, and then overlock. In the same way, join the other edge of each side panel to the two long edges of the remaining panel.

3. For the dowel channels, turn under 1cm (³⁄₈in) on the two shorter edges of each of the eight rectangles; stitch. Now fold in half lengthways, wrong sides together, and press.

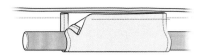

4. Pin the eight dowel channels to the wrong side of the fabric cover along the seam lines at the positions indicated. Stitch in place.

5. Overlock the top edge and the bottom edge. Now press under 1cm (³⁄₈in) on each of these edges and stitch – or, if you prefer, you can press under 5mm (¹⁄₄in) twice and then stitch, to create a double rolled hem.

BALLOON STRINGS

1. Draw balloon strings freehand on to the front left side of the tepee so that the balloons tie in a cluster on the side panel. Sew the narrow ribbon into place over the lines.

2. Finish the balloon strings with a ribbon bow at the base.

TIES

1. For the door ties, press under 1cm (³/₈in) on each long edge and end of the four fabric strips. Press each strip in half lengthways, wrong sides together, and stitch along these edges and ends.

2. Sew one tie on the outside of the cover, at the side seam joining a lower front panel and a side panel, 40cm (16in) above the lower hemmed edge. Sew a second tie to the opening edge of the door, at the same height but on the wrong side of the door. Sew the remaining pair of ties to the other door and side seam. Tie the inner and outer ties together to hold each door in place.

MAT

1. Overlock the edges of the large square, and press under 2cm (³/₄in) on each edge. Pin in place.

2. From scraps of the tepee fabric, cut four 10 × 5cm (4 × 2in) strips. Press edges inwards. Now fold the strip in half crossways and pin one at each corner of the mat, tucking the raw ends under the hem of the mat.

3. Stitch the mat hem on all four edges, catching in the ends of the loops at the same time. Here I've made a simple patchwork mat to the same size.

BUNTING

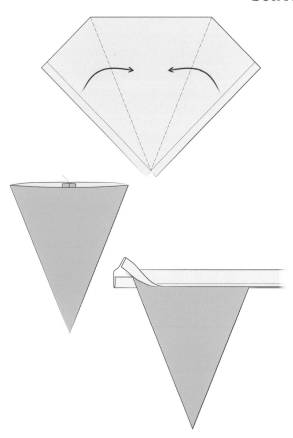

1. For the bunting, cut off the corner of each of the eight 25cm (10in) squares along the line shown on the pattern available online (see page 11), and fold in the remaining two full-length edges along the dotted lines shown on the template. Pin these edges with right sides together and stitch 1cm (³/₈in) from the edge. Press the seam open, turn through and press the folded edges of each double-thickness triangle, with the seam running down the middle.

2. Sandwich the raw edges of each bunting triangle inside the two layers of the length of bias binding, spacing the triangles evenly. Stitch the binding to the triangles, then join the ends of the binding to create a continuous loop.

FLAGS

1. Using the flag pattern available online (see page 11), mark out with tailor's chalk the flag shapes on the coloured fabric, adding 1cm (³/₈in) all around for seam allowances – you'll need two pieces for each flag, and up to four flags. If desired, also cut out a piece of fusible interfacing for each flag.

2. If desired, iron stiff interfacing to one of the pieces for each flag, following the manufacturer's instructions. Pin the two pieces for a flag, with right sides together, around the edges. Stitch, leaving a 4cm (1½in) opening at one corner on the short edge.

3. Turn through and press. Topstitch 4cm (1½in) from the short edge to create a channel for the dowel.

FINISHING

1. Sew a button to each of the seams between panels at the height of the top of the doorway. The bunting will be draped over these.

2. Stitch the ends of the 20cm (8in) length of elastic together to form a loop.

3. Sand the ends of the dowels if necessary, then insert them through the channels on the inside of the tepee cover. Secure the dowels at the top with the loop of elastic, wrapping it tightly over them. Arrange the bottom of each dowel on the floor, putting one through each of the loops at the corners of the mat. You can add rubber feet if you wish, which will help to protect a wooden or tiled floor.

4. Drape the bunting over the buttons, and insert the top of each dowel into the channel on a flag. If desired, wrap webbing tape over the elastic at the top to cover it.

FAVOURITE DOLL

Simple to make, this soft, cuddly doll makes a great gift for either a girl or a boy, as you can personalise the gender and the hair and eye colours, as well as the clothing or trim. Choose fabrics from a wide range of quilter's cottons in geometric prints, or use scraps of fabric or felt, possibly to match garments you've already made for your little one. This project allows you to create a longstanding keepsake. You can also alter the scale of the pattern to create tiny or much larger dolls.

YOU WILL NEED

Girl doll or boy doll patterns

Plain cotton in a skin-tone shade for the legs, arms and face

Scraps of felt or corduroy for the hair

Fabric for dress or top

Fabric for stockings or trousers

Contrast fabric, for the boy doll's shoes and cape

Iron-on double-sided adhesive web or fusible interfacing

Ready-made bias binding (optional) for tie on the cape

Small bag of polyester toy filling (a shoe box size)

Small vintage button (optional)

Embroidery thread (optional)

Matching and contrast sewing thread

Tailor's chalk

CUTTING OUT

This boy doll or girl doll has a stuffed head, body, arms and legs, which are sewn together and decorated as desired.

NOTE: Seam allowances are 1cm (³⁄₈in) unless otherwise specified.

1. Using the girl doll pattern available online (see page 11), prepare the patterns for the face, hair, dress and stockings and arms; or, using the boy doll templates, also available online (see page 11), prepare the patterns for the face, hair, top, trousers, shoes, arms, cape front and cape back.

2. Press the fabric and mark around the pattern pieces using tailor's chalk, adding 1cm (³⁄₈in) all around for seam allowances.

3. From the skin-tone cotton, cut out one head front, and, for the girl doll, two upper legs. From the fabric for the hair, cut one head back. From the fabric for the dress or top, cut out two dress or top pieces. From the fabric for the stockings or trousers, cut out two stocking or trouser pieces. From contrast fabric, cut out two shoe pieces, two cape fronts and one cape back for the boy doll. For the necktie, either cut out one 44 × 3.5cm (17¹⁄₂ × 1¹⁄₂in) strip of bias binding from the contrast fabric, or cut a 44cm (17¹⁄₂in) length of ready-made bias binding.

(CON'T)

FACE & HAIR

1. Bond adhesive web (see page 13) to the wrong side of each piece of fabric for the hair and eyes, and also for glasses or a mask if using.

2. Using the pattern available online (see page 11) draw the shapes on the front of the fabric using tailor's chalk, and cut out.

3. Peel off the backing paper and position the hair and eyes (and glasses or mask if using) on the head front, adhesive side down. Cover with a soft cloth and heat-press in place (see page 13). Topstitch close to the edges of the hair, and for each eye topstitch horizontal lines and then vertical lines to make a cross shape, using a contrast thread.

4. Embroider the mouth on the head front using embroidery thread or a double length of sewing thread.

5. Pin the head front to the head back, right sides together, and stitch, leaving the neck edge unstitched. Snip into the curved seam allowances. Turn through and press.

6. Stuff the head with toy filling, using a pencil to help you push it right to the edge. Do not overfill at this stage.

LEGS & ARMS

1. For the girl doll, pin the lower edge of an upper leg to the top edge of each stocking, right sides together. Stitch and press.

2. For the boy doll, pin a shoe to the lower edge of each leg. Stitch and press.

3. Fold the legs in half lengthways, right sides together, and stitch down the length of each leg and around each foot or shoe, leaving the legs open at the top. Snip into the curved seam allowances, turn through and press.

4. Fold the arms in half lengthways, right sides together, and stitch down the length of each arm and around each hand, leaving the arms open at the top. Snip into the curved seam allowances, turn through and press.

5. Stuff the legs and arms with toy filling, using a pencil to help you push it right to the end.

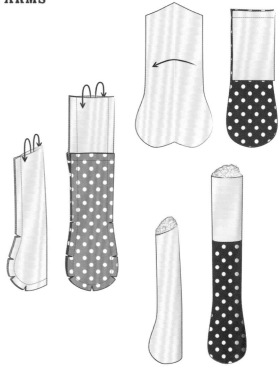

ASSEMBLY

1. Using the template as a guide for placement, pin the arms and legs in position on the right side of the body back (for the boy or girl doll), with raw edges together. Stitch in place.

2. Pin the body front to the body back, right sides together, with the arms and legs between them. Stitch around the outside of the body, leaving the neck edge open. Turn through and press.

3. Pin the head front to the body front at the neck edge, right sides together and raw edges even. Stitch.

4. Add additional filling to the head, and stuff the body, with the remaining toy filling, using a pencil to help you push it right to the ends. Make sure you add plenty of filling at the neck so the head won't be too floppy.

5. Turn under 1cm (³⁄₈in) on the neck edge of the head back and the body back, and slipstitch the folded edges together securely.

TIP
Using felt for the cape and hair is easier because the edges don't need finishing, but woven fabric gives a stronger result.

CAPE

1. For the boy doll's cape, overlock all edges of the cape fronts and back if using fabric; this isn't necessary if using felt. Pin each front to the back at the sides, with right sides together, and stitch the side seams. Press the seams open. Press under a 1cm (³⁄₈in) hem on all edges apart from the neckline; stitch. Add detail depending on your chosen design.

2. For the tie at the neck, press under 5mm (¹⁄₄in) along the long edges of the bias strip, if using. Open out one fold of this strip, or of your ready-made bias binding, and pin the right side of the binding to the wrong side of the cape at the neckline, with raw edges even and an equal amount of the binding extending beyond each centre front edge of the neckline. Stitch around the neckline edge along the crease in the binding.

3. Fold the strip over to the right side of the cape. With the pressed edge turned under, pin the binding to the neckline and topstitch in place, covering the previous stitching. Continue stitching the two pressed-under edges together on both ends of the tie that extend beyond the neckline.

FINISHING

Referring to the pattern, add further detail to your doll, such as a floral hair trim, by cutting the shapes from felt and hand sewing into place. A small vintage button also looks rather sweet here.

PUPPET THEATRE

This puppet theatre will provide endless interactive play. Simple to make, it hangs neatly in a doorway by means of a telescopic net-curtain pole and rolls away compactly between shows. Your children will love hiding behind the window and sharing tales with you or using puppets and toys for endless storytelling. Any woven fabric will work for this, but choose bright colours to stimulate children's imaginations.

YOU WILL NEED

Theatre top panel, bottom panel and side panel patterns

Canopy and star templates

1½m (59in) fabric for theatre

30cm (12in) fabric for curtains

Scraps of 4 contrast fabrics for canopy, bunting and star

30cm (12in) square of iron-on double-sided adhesive web

2m (79in) cotton webbing tape, 3cm (1¼in) wide

2 ribbons, each 46cm (18in) long

2 net-curtain rods to fit 70cm- (27½in-) wide theatre

(or 2 dowels, cut to length and with the ends sanded)

Telescopic curtain pole to fit up to 1m (39in)

Matching sewing thread

Tailor's chalk

CUTTING OUT

This puppet theatre consists of four fabric panels surrounding a window, with curtains tied back at the sides of the window. The theatre is stiffened with net-curtain poles or dowels, and hung in a doorway from a telescopic curtain pole.

NOTE: Seam allowances are 1cm (³⁄₈in) unless otherwise specified.

1. Enlarge the theatre patterns available online (see page 11) by the specified amount and make a pattern for the theatre top panel, bottom panel and side panel. It's a good idea to measure your doorway opening first. The pattern will produce a standard theatre 70cm (27½ in). However do adjust the template and pole sizes accordingly if you prefer a narrower or wider theatre.

2. Press the theatre fabric and arrange it on a flat surface so you can cut out one top panel, one bottom panel and two side panels.

3. Mark around the pattern pieces using tailor's chalk, adding 1cm (³⁄₈in) all around for seam allowances. Cut out the pieces.

4. Press the curtain fabric and cut out two 36 × 51cm (14 × 20in) rectangles from it.

5. Using the canopy pattern, cut out four canopy panels from four contrast fabrics.

(CON'T)

BUNTING

1. From the contrast fabrics, cut out fourteen 10cm (4in) squares

2. Fold each square in half and press. Now fold the two corners that are on the fold towards the opposite raw edges, so the folds meet in the middle and you have a triangle shape. Press again.

3. With raw edges even, pin then sew seven bunting pieces to the lower edge of the theatre.

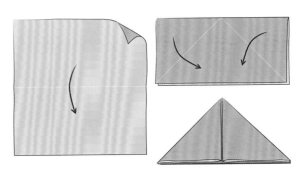

APPLIQUÉ STAR

1. Bond adhesive web to the wrong side of a scrap of fabric for the star (see page 13). Using the template on page 213, draw the star shape on the backing paper, and cut out.

2. Peel off the backing paper and place the star, adhesive side down, at the centre of the bottom theatre panel on the right side. Cover with a soft cloth and heat-press in place. Topstitch close to the edges.

TIP
If you can't source a telescopic curtain pole, you can instead add tab loops to the top corners of the theatre, then suspend them from hooks screwed into the doorframe. However, this does require permanent fixings. Omitting the net-curtain poles or dowels is also possible, but bear in mind that they give structure and shape to the theatre.

APPLIQUÉ CANOPY

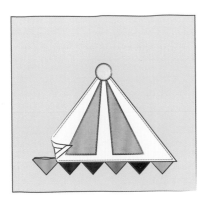

1. Using the pattern, prepare a main canopy triangle adding seam allowance. Press the seam allowance under, pin the triangle to the top theatre panel and sew into place, inserting the remaining bunting triangles into place between the layers.

2. Bond adhesive web (see page 13) to the wrong side of the contrast fabric for the contrast panels and circle. Use the template to trace and cut out four canopy panels, and one circle. Peel away the paper backing. Place the adhesive side into place on to the main canopy. Press into place and topstitch.

ASSEMBLY

1. Overlock all edges of the theatre panels.

2. Join the sides to the top to assemble, and seam together.

3. Turn back all edges by 1cm (³⁄₈in) and sew to finish.

4. Turn back the top of the theatre to create a channel deep enough to insert your telescopic pole.

5. Fold each ribbon tie in half and mark the centre. Sew these into position 10cm (4in) up from the side edges of the window, left and right. This will form the curtain ties.

CURTAINS

1. Overlock all edges of the curtains. Press under 1cm (³⁄₈in) on the side and bottom edges of both curtains, and stitch.

2. Press under the top edge of each curtain by enough to make a casing for your telescopic curtain pole; stitch.

3. To make a casing for the lower net-curtain pole or dowel, cut a length of webbing tape to the width of the theatre. Pin the tape to below the window on the wrong side, and stitch close to the long edges, leaving the ends open, but raw edges turned under. Insert the pole.

4. To hold the telescopic curtain pole and the curtains, cut the remaining webbing tape into three 6cm (2¼ in) lengths. Pin and stitch them to the wrong side of the theatre at the sides, left and right of the theatre window, as shown. Make a third central tab above the window and sew down, creating three tabs into which the pole can be inserted.

FINISHING

1. Insert the net-curtain poles or dowels into the channels at top and bottom and below the window.

2. Insert the telescopic curtain pole through the channel at the top of each of the two curtains.

3. Hang the theatre within the door frame by extending the ends of the telescopic pole to fit, as shown in the manufacturer's instructions for the rod itself.

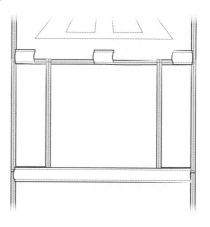

TEMPLATES

All templates need to be increased by 200% unless otherwise stated in the pattern.

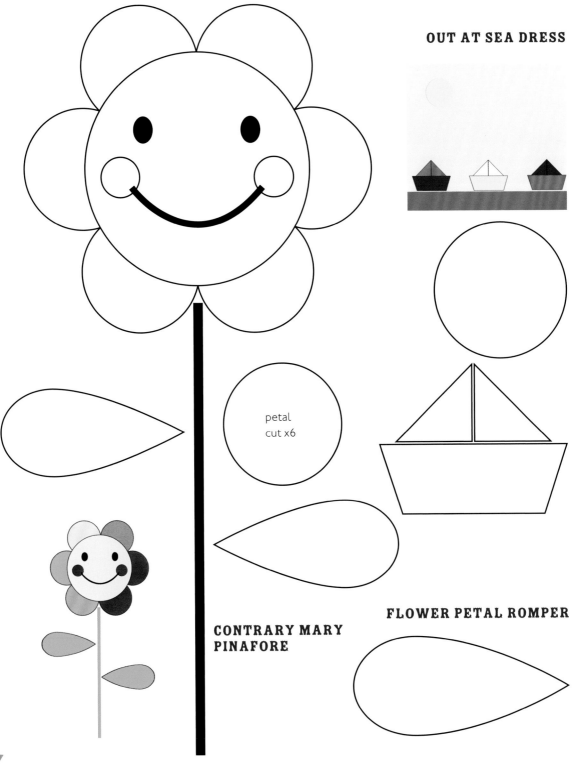

OUT AT SEA DRESS

petal
cut x6

**CONTRARY MARY
PINAFORE**

FLOWER PETAL ROMPER

BALLOON PARTY DRESS & PARTY TEPEE

Print +300% for Party Tepee

MERMAID STORYTIME SUNDRESS

BAT HOODIE

LITTLE CHICK REVERSIBLE APRON

BUNNY RABBIT CHARACTER DRESS & ANIMAL EARS CUSHION

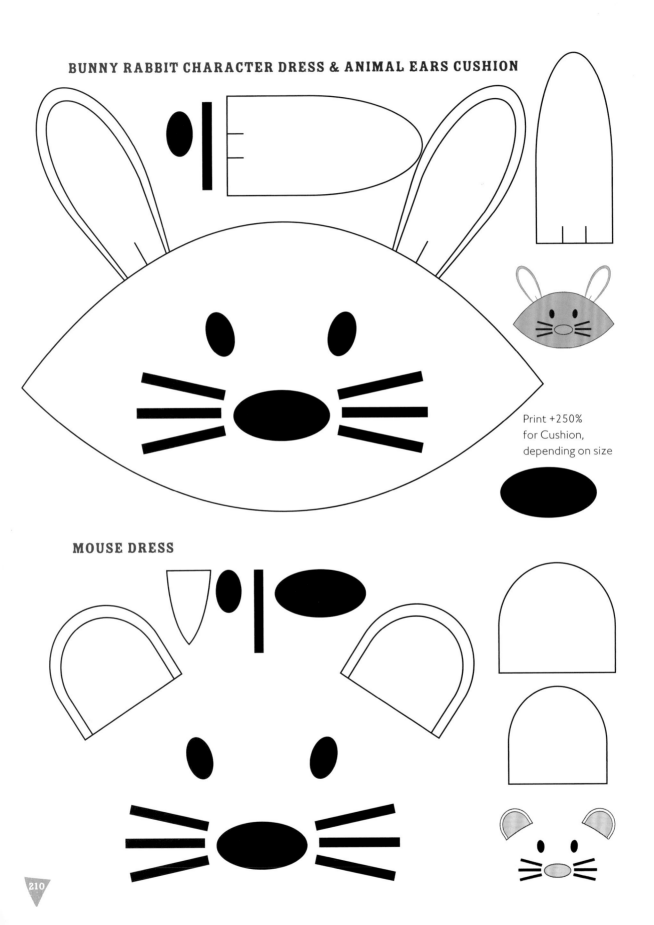

Print +250% for Cushion, depending on size

MOUSE DRESS

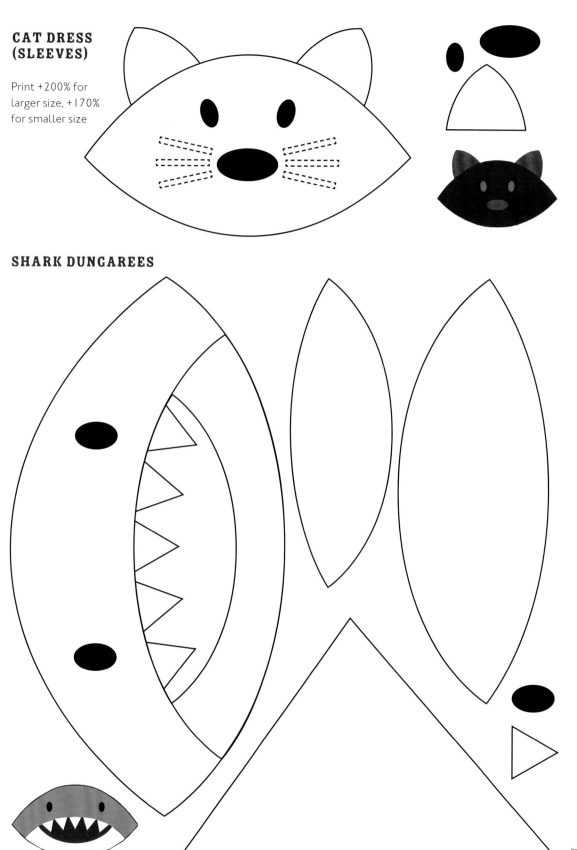

CAT DRESS (SLEEVES)

Print +200% for larger size, +170% for smaller size

SHARK DUNGAREES

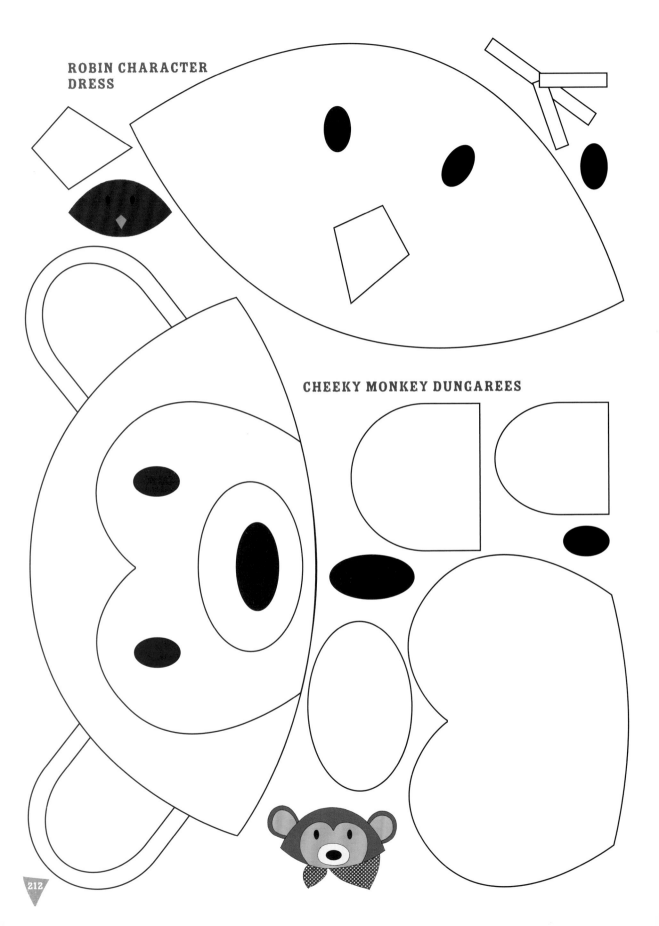

ROBIN CHARACTER
DRESS

CHEEKY MONKEY DUNGAREES

212

TEDDY BEAR CHARACTER CAPE

GO-FASTER SUPERHERO CAPE AND CAP SET & PUPPET THEATRE

Print +250% for
Puppet Theatre

DOGHOUSE SWEATSHIRT

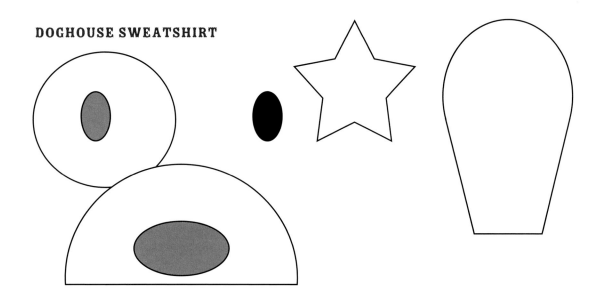

REVERSIBLE KITTY TODDLER TROUSERS & ANIMAL EARS CUSHION

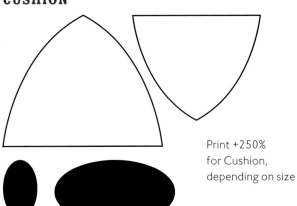

Print +250% for Cushion, depending on size

HIPPY CHICK FEATHER SUN TOP

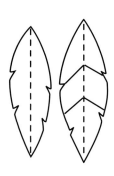

BABY HAREM DUNGAREES

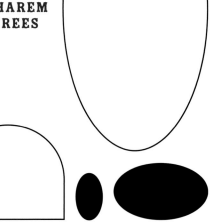

PRINCESS CAPE

PARTY TEPEE

LITTLE MISSY
THEATRE COAT

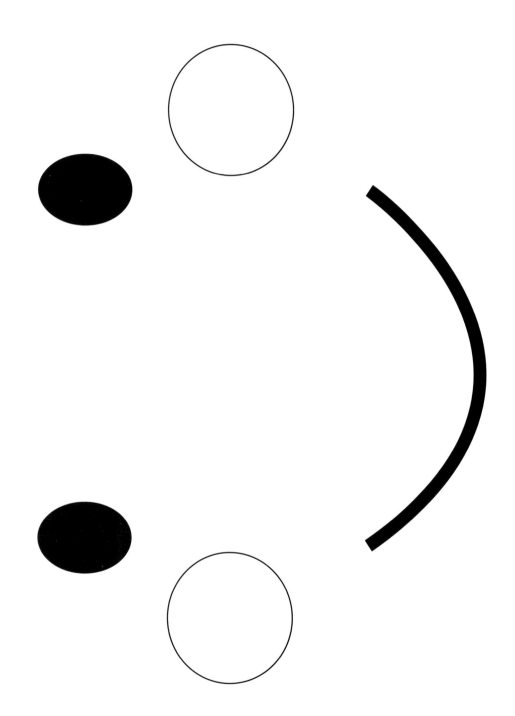

GLOSSARY

Appliqué
This term comes from the French word for 'to apply'. In sewing terms, to apply shape and pattern using one fabric to another.

Backstitch
Also known as reverse stitching, this provides extra durability at the start and end of a seam or line of stitching.

Baste
To roughly join together two fabrics or layers before sewing. Sewing threads are removed later. Also known as tacking.

Bias
Fabric cut on the bias is cut at a 45-degree angle to the selvedge or finished fabric edge.

Binding
This is the technique of creating a decorative border to finish an edge, using pre-prepared or self-made fabric, often bias-binding.

Blindstitch
A stitch often used on a garment hem that is invisible, achieved by working against a folded edge, carefully catching or picking the edge of the fold with the needle and sewing so that the thread is concealed.

Edge stitching
Stitching close to an edge to secure appliqué or provide a neat finish.

Ease
Gently allowing one longer seam to match another when sewing, by 'easing' into place, usually when sewing curved or gathered edges.

Finish
Overall presentation and appearance, achieved with good practice and careful handle, especially through pressing. Refers also to a treatment of a fabric such as a coating or brush 'finish'.

Fat quarter
A fat quarter refers to a quarter yard of quilting fabric, often quilter's cotton, measuring 45cm (18in)×55cm (22in), assuming that the fabric is 110cm (44in) wide. Refer to each project for required fabric quantities or to the measurements of the child, which are given in both metric and imperial measurements.

Face
Refers to the top, correct, or 'right side' of the fabric.

Facing
This is an inner layer of fabric, cut to form a finished edge and strengthen the main body of a garment.

French seam
A seam in which all raw edges are trapped by sewing twice.

Fold line
Refers to a marking on a pattern that requires you to place the pattern on to a folded piece of fabric, when the opposite side of the folded area is symmetrical.

Gather
Easing, or runching, one fabric to another to create a gathered finish.

Grain line
The grain line is marked on the pattern piece as a long arrow, normally parallel to the centre front or centre back of the garment. It indicates where to place the pattern on the fabric.

Hems
The lower edge of a garment that requires hand or machine stitching to finish.

Notch
A marking on a pattern piece that denotes where it, and a corresponding notch on another pattern piece, are intended to be placed together, rather like a jigsaw puzzle.

Overlock
A specific machine stitch that will finish and trim simultaneously to eliminate raw edges

Pile or nap

Refers to fabrics with a raised pile such as velvet or corduroy, which have a clear direction to the way the pile lies, meaning you will need to cut everything with the pile running in the same direction.

Pressing

Use of a good-quality steam iron, to prepare and finish a garment, often 'pressing' seams open.

Raw edge

This is the unfinished edge of cut fabric.

Right sides together / RS facing

This refers to when the face or right sides of the fabrics are placed together before sewing.

Rouleau loop

A loop made from bias-cut fabric, used to loop around a button to form a fastening.

Seam

A seam is made when two fabrics are sewn with edges together.

Seam allowance

The additional fabric between the sewing line and the edge of the fabric.

Satin stitch

A flush smooth finish created by sewing back and forth close together along an edge. Can be used to hand sew buttonholes.

Selvedge

Refers to the finished edge of the fabric running along the warp of a woven fabric.

Snipping curves

Cutting into curved seam allowances to create a better finish and reduce bulk.

Tack or baste

Hand sewing to temporarily secure layers in place, which helps with fine work. Tacking threads are removed after sewing.

Topstitch

Topstitching can be used for decorative purposes but more often it is used to achieve a flat and strong edge finish. Often in a contrast colour.

Understitch

Strengthens and neatens edges. Rather than topstitch, understitching cannot be seen from the face of the garment . Sew close to the edge on the inside of the garment with all seam allowances pressed to the inside of the garment.

Warp

In woven fabrics, runs lengthways parallel to the selvedge.

Weft

In woven fabrics, runs widthways at 45-degrees to the selvedge.

Wrong side

Refers to the reverse, back, or 'wrong side' of the fabric.

Zigzag stitch

A stitch setting that moves the needle from left to right rather than in a straight line. Can be used to neaten a raw edge where an overlock is not available, or to create a stretch stitch.

INDEX

STOCKISTS

Remember to always shop local whenever you can!

FOR CORDUROY, & WILD THINGS EXCLUSIVE FABRICS

www.wildthingsdresses.com
www.wildthingstosew.com

FOR A COOL SELECTION OF THE BEST QUILTER'S COTTONS

Fancy Moon: www.fancymoon.co.uk
Fabric Rehab: http://fabricrehab.co.uk
Seamstar: http://www.seamstar.co.uk

PRINT HOUSES:

Review their ranges and buy from your local retailer
Michael Miller Fabrics: www.michaelmillerfabrics.com
Alexander Henry Fabrics: www.ahfabrics.com

FOR BEAUTIFUL CONTEMPORARY WOVEN & JERSEY PRINTS

Monaluna: www.monaluna.com

FOR TRIMS & SUPPLIES

Etsy.com: www.etsy.com/uk/browse/craft-supplies
Barnyarns: www.barnyarns.co.uk

MACHINES

Brother Sewing Machnes: www.brothersewing.co.uk

ACKNOWLEDGEMENTS

A huge thank you to my Publisher Amanda Harris and Editor Jillian Young, for clarity and wisdom, and the outstanding team at Orion Books, including Mark McGinlay. Also to designer Gemma Wilson, who shared the vision and drive to create this book. Thank you to my agent Clare Hulton for continued support and guidance.

Thank you especially to duo Will Shaddock and Jen Murdoch for their inspiring photography and styling. Also to Jamie Tozer and Tom Nichols. To my little muses, Silva and Lila, and models, Libby, Charlotte, Harmony, Skye, Logan and Christopher, for making the shoots such fun. To Rowan Hoban and Sarah Bird of Wild Rumpus for the shoot location and creating the best children's festival, Just So.

To craft author Kat Goldin and Kat Molesworth @thatkat for inspiring and connecting the creative online community. To Charlie Moorby, Lara Watson and the teams at Mollie Makes and Simply Sewing.

To Fritha Tigerlilly Quinn, Emily Quinton and Elena Rosa Brown. To dedicated makers passionate about creating for their own children, including Jill Griffiths and Mindy Scheltens.

To sample maker Linda Young for her skilled dedication to Wild Things, and for championing UK skilled manufacture. To Michelle, Seema, Zoe, Ruby and Rhiannon. To Lynsey Beaton at Standfast and Barracks, Debbie Wilson and Paul Ellison.

And most importantly, thank you to my friends and family: partner Gary, mum Sandra, sisters Cara and Ceri for believing in me, and for endless encouragement and support through late nights and long weekends.

CREDITS

Will Shaddock and
Jen Murdoch :
www. willshaddock.co.uk

PeePow Shoes : http://
www.peepowshoes.com/

Brother Sewing Machines
Europe
GmbH – UK Branch
www.brothersewing.co.uk

First published in Great Britain in 2016
by Orion Books,
an imprint of The Orion Publishing Group Ltd

Carmelite House
50 Victoria Embankment
London EC4Y 0DZ
An Hachette UK Company

10 9 8 7 6 5 4 3 2 1

Designer: Gemma Wilson
Photographer: Will Shaddock
Prop stylist: Jen Murdoch
Illustrator: Kuo Kang Chen
Project editor: Jillian Young
Copy editor: Alison Wormleighton
Proofreader: Beth Dymond
Indexer: Rosemary Dear

A CIP catalogue record for this book is available from the British Library.

ISBN: 978 0 297 87127 9

Printed in China

The Orion Publishing Group's policy is to use papers that are natural,
renewable and recyclable and made from wood grown in sustainable
forests. The logging and manufacturing processes are expected to
conform to environmental regulations of the country of origin.

www.orionbooks.co.uk